What's it about and who's it 4?

Boys are supposed to think about sex once every 30 seconds and girls once a minute – or so the story goes. More myth than fact, perhaps, but it does show what a very important part sex plays in our lives. But you shouldn't believe everything you read in the papers…Most teenagers may start sexual activities like snogging and touching each other up at around 13 or 14 years of age, but even in today's 'sex mad' world three out of four girls and two out of three men are still virgins at the age of 16.

So what have we here in this book? What we can say for sure is that young people want to know more about sex, because we have had literally tens of thousands of emails from young people themselves telling us what they find funny about sex, what they find stimulating about sex, what they find frightening about sex. These emails have been sent to our website **www.teenagehealthfreak.org**, along with truckloads of other emails on drugs, diets, illnesses, relationships – and a thousand other health-related issues.

We have answered young people's emails as honestly as we can, using frank language but without going 'over the top'. What is the size of the average boy's penis? Why do boys like looking at girls' breasts? What happens during sexual intercourse? What does it mean to be 'gay'? These and a million other questions are what young people are faced with as they grow up. The very number of questions asked indicates that young people find this source of information invaluable. Rather than limiting this information to just those who have access to our website, we are now publishing a selection of the best and most useful questions and answers here in book form.

AIDAN MACFARLANE is a consultant paediatrician and public health doctor who ran the child and adolescent health services for Oxfordshire. He is now a freelance international consultant in teenage health.

ANN McPHERSON is a general practitioner with extensive experience of young people and their problems. She is also a lecturer in the Department of Primary Health Care at the University of Oxford.

As well as *The Diary of a Teenage Health Freak* and its sequel *The Diary of the Other Health Freak*, their other books include *Mum I Feel Funny* (which won the Times Education Supplement Information Book Award), *Me and My Mates*, *The Virgin Now Boarding*, and *Fresher Pressure*. They also published a book for parents about the teenage years called *Teenagers: the agony, the ecstasy, the answers*. Their most recent books have been *R U a Teenage Health Freak?* and *Teenage Health Freak: Drugs*, a companion to this book. The authors also run the extremely successful website on which this book is based – **www.teenagehealthfreak.org** – which receives around 250,000 hits a week and recently won the BUPA communication award.

Authors' acknowledgements
We would like to thank: all the teenagers who emailed us – whether we were able to answer them or not – and all their parents for having them in the first place; Liz and the rest of the team at Baigent for their work on the website; Mike and Jane O'Regan for all their support and their funding; Ben Dupré for all his wonderful patience and 'suspect' sense of humour when helping us with the editing. We would also like to thank all the sources of information we have used, including: – the fpa (Family Planning Association), the Brook Advisory Services, John Coleman and The Trust for the Study of Adolescence, David Jones, Liz Greenhall, Chris Donovan, Patrick Horner, John Gillebaud, the Cochrane Collaboration and the Oxford Textbook of Medicine.

Note
The answers we have given to the questions in this book are based on our personal clinical experiences as doctors when dealing with similar clinical problems. Young people reading the book will, we think, be helped by the answers that we have given. However, it is impossible for us to offer advice in such a way as to deal with all aspects of every individual's health problem. Therefore if you, as a reader of this book, have any continuing doubts or concerns about your health problem, we would strongly advise you to consult your own medical practitioner.

To preserve the true flavour of the originals, we have not changed or edited the language or spelling of the emailed questions used in this book. However, in the few cases where real names are used, these have been changed to protect the anonymity of the senders.

the truth

S**E**X

OXFORD
UNIVERSITY PRESS

Great Clarendon Street, Oxford OX2 6DP

Oxford University Press is a department of the University of Oxford.
It furthers the University's objective of excellence in research, scholarship,
and education by publishing worldwide in

Oxford New York

Auckland Cape Town Dar es Salaam Hong Kong Karachi
Kuala Lumpur Madrid Melbourne Mexico City Nairobi
New Delhi Shanghai Taipei Toronto

With offices in

Argentina Austria Brazil Chile Czech Republic France Greece
Guatemala Hungary Italy Japan Poland Portugal Singapore
South Korea Switzerland Thailand Turkey Ukraine Vietnam

Oxford is a registered trade mark of Oxford University Press
in the UK and in certain other countries

British Library Cataloguing in Publication Data available

ISBN 978-0-19-911171-8

3 5 7 9 10 8 6 4

Printed in Great Britain
by Cox & Wyman Ltd., Reading, Berkshire

Third-party website addresses referred to in this publication are
provided by Oxford University Press in good faith and for information
only. Oxford University Press disclaims any responsibility for the material
contained therein.

Contents

What's it all about...?

Sex is much more than having orgasms and babies. OK, it is about having fun and enjoying it, but it's also about respect, trust, friendship, affection, play, love, passion, anger, making up, giggling, etc. – all the vast array of emotions you get in real everyday living.

In fact, the most important, delicious, wonderful, sexy, erogenous zone isn't between your legs – it's that hefty thing inside your head called a brain. This is because sex is always tied up with how we feel about ourselves, how we feel about other people, and how we feel about the world in general. With some people their sexual feelings are made up of pure lust, with other people sexual feelings are tied up with their religious feelings, while with other people it is linked with their feelings of confidence, but with most people it will be a combination of all these things and many others as well.

Like so many other things in life, we don't normally get it right the first time – things can and do go wrong. Relationships fall apart, people fall out of love, people get bored with sex, people get forced into doing things that they don't want to do, people change their mind.

It is therefore good to have some idea about the ups and downs and the ins and outs ahead of time. This will help you know what it is that you want, what you like doing, when you want to do it and when you don't want to do it, and especially who you want to do it with.

This book is there to help you get a feel for all of this.

1 Relationships
getting the chemistry right

Relationships, whether sexual or not, are slippery – one moment they are wonderful, the next they can be a disaster. But if you never try them, then you will never know just how wonderful (or just how awful) they can be. Almost everyone has them – some have more than others. A few people will fall in love immediately and live happily ever after; others will try hundreds of relationships and they will never fall in love. However, most of us will be somewhere in between, trying a series of different relationships and then settling down with one person.

● **WILL ANYBODY EVER LOVE ME?**

Dear Doc – **How can I make better friends with the opposite sex?** Boy age 14.

8

Dear 'Wanting to make better friends with the opposite sex' – Boys want to be friends with girls, and girls with boys, and both can feel quite shy and embarrassed about it. This is mainly because, in order to get more confident at it, you have to get some practice in. Don't try and leap every fence with one bound. Take it easy – find some common interest with the girl and take it from there – but don't rush it. Just try and get a gentle feeling for what is right as you go along.

Dear Dr Ann – **I'm worried that boys don't like me.** Girl aged 14.

Dear 'Worried that boys don't like me' – Most girls worry whether boys like them and, in just the same way, most boys tend to worry whether girls like them too. So there is a lot of worrying going on. It may seem as though all your girl friends find it easy to talk to boys, as some girls appear more confident than others, but even they probably worry about it. It's best to remember that boys are just as nervous and worried as you are. Find some simple common interests, concentrate on having good friends, whether they are girls or boys, learn to like yourself and I'm sure boys will like you.

Dear Dr Ann – **I can't chat up girls.** I'm too shy and I wonder if I will ever find the courage to chat up girls and ask girls out. I can talk to girls and have some girl mates, but I can't ever chat them up. Boy aged 15.

Dear 'Too shy' – We *all* find it difficult at times to 'chat up' someone of the opposite sex, particularly someone we fancy. Girls will be just as nervous as you. The best thing is to start talking to girls (which you seem to be very good at) about things that you have in common, and then slowly, slowly get around to showing them that you fancy them. If you are moving too fast, they will hopefully let you know in a very nice way – so don't be afraid.

Hi Dr Ann – **I have no boyfriend but I really want one.** This is because I want someone to hang around with me, hold my hand and be there for me when i am down or 'on'. I don't know how you could help but could you please try as i am getting really down. Maybe give me some tips to help me get one. I dunno, but you're the doc and I don't know you which makes it easier to ask you. Thank you. Girl age 15.

Dear 'Really wanting a boyfriend to hang around with' – We all want a really good supportive friend, but the best relationships and friendships need to be equal, not just one person wanting a prop for when they are down. Unfortunately, there is no instant solution to finding a boyfriend. The first tip is to start making friends with boys and girls and then you might meet someone who you like and likes you. The second tip is to relax and let it happen. The next tip is to stop wanting someone to support you, and start wanting someone who you can enjoy being with and who you might support in some way. If you come over as needy and desperate when trying to find the right boyfriend, it is much less likely to happen.

Dear Dr Ann – **I don't usually have much luck with boys, but one asked me out 2 weeks ago** and now because I'm not used to this kind of thing, everytime I'm around him I get nervous 'n when I get nervous I go all quiet and now I think that he's starting to think I don't like him what do I do??? Its really getting me down as I cant seem to stop it or tell him!! 14 year old girl.

> *Dear 'Without luck with boys'* – It sounds as if you have struck lucky here, but are getting over-anxious about it all. Don't be too worried about being a bit quiet – most boys quite like to have someone to listen to them. It is very likely he is nervous too. Listen carefully to what he says and pick up on something he says that interests you and that you think you know something about. Before you realize it, you will be carrying on a conversation and will forget about being nervous.

Dear Doc – **I went out with my best friend's girlfriend and now he refuses to talk to me what can i do.** Boy aged 14.

> *Dear 'Girlfriend snatcher'* – I'm not surprised that your best friend is no longer your best friend. Being a best friend means respecting another person, thinking about them, considering their feelings and wanting them to be happy. So going out with your best friend's girlfriend can only mean that you are thinking of yourself rather than what it means to be a good friend. If you really want to be his friend again, you'll have to say you are sorry, and mean it and explain why it happened.

11

Dr Ann — **I am a 13 year old girl and currently have never kissed.** At the moment I don't have a boyfriend. If a guy friend asks me to kiss him, should I, or wait to see if we start a relationship?

Dear 'Should I kiss a guy?' – If the guy is really a friend, then maybe it is OK to kiss, but it's always good to wait and only start kissing someone with whom you have a relationship. There's a saying 'Treat them mean keep them keen!' So don't go round kissing any guy friend who asks!

Dear Doctor Ann — **Hi I like this boy from my school and I think he likes me a bit.** I phone him and he sometimes phones me back. Anyway I really like him and want to ask him to come out to the pictures or something with me. How shall I ask him???? 15 female.

Dear 'Wanting to ask a boy out' – There's no rule that says it's the boy that has to ask the girl out rather than the other way round. Why not pluck up courage and when he next phones ask him? Or, if you were feeling a bit braver, you could phone him. If he has a mobile phone, you could text message him. But remember, he might say 'yes' or he might say 'no' – and if it's the latter, it might be because he is shy or not ready to go out on his own with girls – so you could always suggest going out in a crowd.

Dear doctor Ann — **I am in love with this boy who gets my train.** He is in the year below me but he looks fairly old. I know he has got a lovely personality. He is a real gentleman. I have tried asking him out and I explained how I felt in a letter but he said that he didn't fancy me. I really do love him. Nothing will ever change it. I feel he is the one. Female 14.

> *Dear 'In love with a boy on the train'* – You seem to be attracted to him, obsessed by him and infatuated by him, but this does not mean that this is love. Love is a funny old mixture of friendship, respect, trust, lust, affection etc., but you have to know a person really well before you can tell whether you have all these together! So, if you really like this guy, lay off pursuing him – he may become a friend, but he has been rightly very honest with you about how he feels. Realize your feelings for what they are, develop friendships with other boys, and sooner or later you will really fall in love with someone who feels the same way about you.

● THE AGONY WHEN IT GOES WRONG

Dear Doctor — **Can u please help me. I have just split up with my girlfriend after 3 and a half weeks because she said i was boring** and now I have got this really weird feeling I just want to cry all the time and I really want 2 get back together do you think there is any chance? Do you have any ideas about what I can do. Please e-mail me back i need help thanks. Boy aged 16.

> *Dear 'Wanting to cry all the time'* – Ouch! – welcome to the real world. I am afraid that you are suffering, and suffering in a way that we all suffer when we find

13

someone that we really want as a partner. The simple answer is 'yes' – there is always a chance. I know lots of young people who have been together for a time, then split up, and then come together again, so don't give up – but 3½ weeks is a very short time to fully test out a relationship. If she is already bored with it and you, better for you to find someone new who does appreciate you.

Dear Dr Ann – **Me and my boyfriend (of a year and 8 months) have just split up.** I am in so much pain and I just wondered if you had any advice except 'it takes time'. Anything to keep me busy or just ANYTHING. Female 15.

Dear 'Just split up' – Splitting up is usually painful at the time, even if it is the right thing to do. But now that you have done the splitting, in some ways you have got the worst over with. There are positives to splitting up if it is the right thing to do. Time is going to be the thing which helps most – but there are things you can do to help yourself. Make a list of the good things about splitting – you will have time to see other friends, you'll be able to meet new people, try new things that your old boyfriend might not have been interested in. The pain will go away, and in a few months' time you may well be pleased that this has happened.

Boys' changes

getting your
equipment
ready

Some guys look like gorillas by the time they're 12; others are just starting to get their first pubic hairs at 14. Everyone grows at different rates, but we all eventually go through puberty and all grow into adults. The changes at puberty are caused by the release of hormones. Hormones are chemical messengers made by one part of the body, like the brain or your balls (testes), and which affect another bit of the body. Although there are many different 'sex' hormones, they have got to work together to make puberty happen.

● **ALL CHANGE**

Dear Doctor Ann – **What's the earliest age you can start puberty?** 12 year old boy.

15

Dear 'Age of puberty wonderer'– Around the age of 8 years is a fair estimate, although very occasionally it may start even earlier. On the whole, over the last 50 years or so, boys and girls have tended to start puberty earlier and earlier, but this 'earlier' start now seems to be slowing up a bit! Generally, boys tend to worry more about starting too 'late' rather than starting too 'early'!

Hi Doctor Ann – **What do you do if you are not going through puberty?** 14 year old boy.

Dear 'Wanting to start puberty'– There is a huge range of ages at which boys start going through their puberty. It can start as early as 8 years, or as late as 15 years, and still be all completely normal – just as some people are tall and some are short. Be patient and wait a bit longer. The first signs of puberty are normally your testes (balls) growing bigger, and your scrotum (ball sac) growing. This is then normally followed by you beginning to get a few wispy pubic hairs. It will happen – but if nothing at all has started by the time you are 15, then you should go and talk to your doctor about it and get your hormones checked out.

Dear Doctor Ann – **I'm 14 and all my friends voices have broken but mine hasn't. It's really embarrassing** because not many people believe my age and all my 14-year-old friends can pass as 15 for films and stuff. I used to be one of the tallest in my year when I was younger, but now everyone is overtaking and I'm one of the smallest. I know it's because I haven't reached puberty yet, but is there any way of speeding up the process because it seems I'll be like this forever. Please help. 14 year old boy.

Dear 'Anxious to speed up puberty' – Please, please be patient. As you say, your turn will come. You will only have to put up with being shorter than your friends for a short time and then your growth spurt will begin. I do understand how difficult it must be when your friends have begun to have deeper voices and yours still remains 'high' – but again, it will all be OK in a very short time. There are no exercises you can do with your voice or other parts of your body to make puberty start earlier – your body has its own timing for these things. Going to see a doctor at this stage would be a waste of time – she/he would only tell you to be patient, too. Don't worry about the girls – you will find yourself surrounded in due course as their hormones begin to recognize your hormones.

BODY – HEIGHT, SHOULDERS, FACE AND VOICE

👁 9–12 years (average 10ish):	*your hormones start the changes*
👁 9–15 years (average 12–13):	*your body grows and changes shape*
👁 11–16 years (average 13–14):	*growing fast – you grow up to a quarter of your final height during this time! Shoulders get wider, your muscles get heavier.*
👁 11–17 years (average 14–15):	*your skin gets more oily, leading to spots. Your voice breaks.*
👁 14–18 years (average 16ish):	*you are nearly adult height and build*

Dear Dr Ann – **When will I have a growth spurt?** 13 year old boy.

Dear 'Growing worrier' – Puberty actually begins at very different ages in different boys. Your growth spurt, which is part of puberty, may actually occur at any time between 10 and 15 years of age, and sometimes you may go on growing in height even until you are 20.

● **HAIR – PUBIC, CHIN, CHEST AND UNDERARM**

- 👁 *9–12 years (average 10ish):*   you have no pubic or under-arm hair
- 👁 *9–15 years (average 12–13):*   you get a little fine wispy hair at the base of the penis
- 👁 *11–16 years (average 13–14):*   pubic hair looks like adult's, although there's not so much of it
- 👁 *11–17 years (average 14–15):*   underarm and leg hair grows, and wispy hair appears on chin and upper lip
- 👁 *14–18 years (average 16ish):*   more hair on face – shaving soon, which turns it to bristles. Some guys have chest hair.

Dear Doctor Ann – **How can i speed up the process of developing facial hair?** 16 year old boy.

Dear 'Facial hair grower' – There is no easy way to speed up the growth of your facial hair. The growth of hair on your face happens fairly late in puberty. So, if your testes (balls) have started getting bigger, and your ball sac has started to grow, and you have started to get pubic hair, then it is likely that the growth of hair on your face is not far behind.

Dear Doctor Ann – **Should I have pubic hair at my age?** 17 year old boy.

Dear '17-year-old wondering about pubic hair' – Yes, you should have pubic hair by the age of 17 – even if it has not fully developed to be coarse and black and curly. If you haven't got any pubic hair at all, you need to go and see your doctor about it and discuss what investigations you may need. A very small number of boys will need hormone treatment to bring their puberty on if it is very late in happening.

● CHANGES IN PENISES AND BALLS (TESTES)

● *9–12 years (average 10ish):*	balls (testes) are getting ready to start growing
● *9–15 years (average 12–13):*	balls and scrotum double in size (they'll get 7 times bigger eventually!) but penis doesn't grow much
● *11–16 years (average 13–14)*	balls are getting bigger. Penis gets longer but not much wider.
● *11–17 years (average 14–15):*	balls are still growing – big enough to produce the 100 million sperm that leak each time you have a wet dream (which happen around now). Penis gets thicker and longer.
● *14–18 years (average 16ish):*	balls and penis become full grown-up size

Dear Doctor Ann — **How do you know when your balls have dropped?** 14 year old boy.

Dear 'Waiting for balls to drop' – One of the early signs of starting puberty is when your balls begin to grow larger, and at the same time your 'ball sac' also begins to grow bigger. However, often boys' testes often don't hang fully down till towards the end of puberty – which may be as late as 17 years of age. So you can see it is a gradual process and not one that happens overnight. It is different in different boys – just look around in the showers at school!

Dear Doctor Ann — **When will my sperm start to grow?** 11 year old boy.

Dear 'Sperm grower' – Making sperm is the job of your testes (balls). To work really well, your testes have to be kept at a slightly cooler temperature than the rest of your body, which is why they hang outside in their own sac. Control over when your balls make sperm is via two hormones called testosterone and follicular stimulating hormone. These are also produced by your testes themselves. But production of these two 'male' hormones by your testes is controlled from your brain. The exact timing of when your brain turns these hormones on at the beginning of your puberty varies. Why some boys start puberty early on, around the age of 8, or later on, around the age of 15, is still not clear.

Dear Doc — **I am very worried about the size of my penis. I'm 15 and it is only about an inch long when not erect.** i don't think this is normal for a 15 year old boy. I don't think i have started puberty yet – my voice hasn't broken, i have no underarm hair and i have hardly any hair around my penis. I am very worried because my friend's penis is very big and he is 14. I am older and even though I haven't started puberty i think i should be bigger by now. But aren't I very late? I think every boy in my year has started to shave because they have facial hair. I have never needed to shave in my life!! Well actually if u know any way to get my penis bigger I would be very grateful. Thanks.

Dear '15-year-old with very few pubertal changes' – You do appear to be having your puberty at the 'late' end of normal. If you are quite far into your 16th year, then you should go and consult your doctor. Don't worry too much, because if you are slow in starting your puberty, it is unlikely that there is anything seriously wrong. If there is an actual problem, however, then you may need treatment with some special hormones that your doctor can prescribe and which will 'bring on' your puberty. Your penis will then grow bigger.

3 Girls' changes
getting started

Most of girls' pubertal changes take place between the ages of 10 and 15. The changes are due to 'hormones' – chemical messengers made by one part of the body (like the brain or the ovary) which affect another bit of the body. No one is exactly sure why the body starts to produce these sex hormones around this time. Some of these hormones are involved in sex, and without them, periods wouldn't happen, babies wouldn't grow up, we wouldn't want sex, girls wouldn't release an egg each month and the fertilized egg would never develop into a baby.

The chief female sex hormones are oestrogen and progesterone. They are mainly produced in the ovaries, but their production is controlled by hormones from the brain. The ovaries in women also make a small amount of the male sex hormone – testosterone. Men make 10 times as much testosterone as women, and women make 10 times more oestrogen and progesterone than men.

Dear Dr – Hi, this is SO embarrassing and if anyone found out I would have 2 move schools, but the problem is **I have no pubic hair, boobs, underarm hair, periods etc.** I'm 14 and all my friends have everything. Is there anything the doctor can do to speed up the process? please help! from embarrassed 14 year old girl.

> *Dear 'Highly embarrassed'* – There is a huge range of ages at which all the things that you are worrying about – pubic hair, boobs, underarm hair, and periods – start to happen. I doubt that every one of your friends have 'everything' yet, and even if all your friends do, look around the rest of your class and there's likely to be someone at the same stage as you. Be patient and it will start to happen.

Dear Ann – **I haven't had any pubic hair grow around my vagina yet and I need to know why.** 15 year old girl.

> *Dear 'Pubic hairless'* – Luckily, we are all different. Some of us are taller or shorter, some fatter or thinner. This also applies to when we get pubic hair, which usually starts to grow any time between the ages of 10 and 15. In some girls it happens earlier, and in others it may be later. If you haven't started getting any pubic hair when you are 15, it would be a  good idea to see your doctor to get checked. There is unlikely to be anything wrong, but a check of your hormones should help sort things out.

Dear Dr Ann – **I share a room with my 10 year old sister and I've noticed that she has got bigger breasts and more pubic hair than me.** I am worried that I am not developing at the right rate as she is younger but more mature than me. 13 year old girl.

Dear '13-year-old with more developed younger sister' – Even though they are in the same family, sisters can go through puberty and develop at different rates. It sounds as though this is true in your case. You are developing at the right rate for you, and she is developing at the right rate for her. Just because these things have happened to her first, it does not mean she is more mature in other ways. Don't worry – your breasts, pubic hair, and underarm hair will all happen to you soon, along with all the other changes of puberty.

● **ARRIVAL OF PUBIC HAIR AND PERIODS**

Dear Dr Ann – **I have just noticed a browny reddy colour in my knickers.** I am not sure if this is my periods starting? 14 year old girl.

Dear 'Coloured knickers' – It does sound as though your hormones are gearing up and that your periods will start soon. You may have a bit of discharge for a few months until the hormones are really working properly. When this happens, you will have a regular cycle, with your body releasing an egg from your ovaries each month. In some girls periods start to happen every month; in others they come every few months to begin with.

Pubic hair and periods

- **8–11 years:** no outside signs yet, but ovaries (the egg producers) are enlarging and hormones are at work

- **8–14 (average 11–12) years:** fine, straight pubic hairs appear

- **9–15 (average 12–13) years:** pubic hair coarsens and becomes darker, but doesn't spread. The vagina may begin to produce a clear or whitish discharge, and means a girl can expect periods within a year. Some girls get their periods – others have to wait a while.

- **10–16 (average 13–14) years:** periods start, usually irregularly at first. Pubic hair starts to grow into the triangular shape of adulthood.

- **12–19 (average 15) years:** periods happen regularly at around monthly intervals, and the ovaries start to release an egg each month

Dear Dr Ann – **I'm 17 and I still haven't had a period – what is wrong?** 17 year old girl.

Dear '17-year-old with no periods' – Most girls have started their periods by the age of 17. Your periods do seem to be rather late coming on and I think it would be wise for you to see your doctor to get checked out. The doctor will want to do some investigations – like blood tests and X-rays of your bones – to see what is going on. But don't worry – if it is a hormone thing, you may be able to take hormones to bring on your periods.

Dear Dr Ann – **I have been getting white patches on my knickers for 2 years and i still have not started my period – what is going on?** 11 year old girl.

Dear 'White patches on your knickers' – Your hormones are starting to work and are sending messages to the glands in your vagina. These glands produce a small amount of discharge and this helps keep your vagina healthy. The discharge is usually clear or slightly milky, or might even be slightly yellow when it dries on your knickers. I would guess that your periods will start soon.

Hiya Dr Ann – **I'm really worried cuz I haven't come on yet and i know that when u first start u r irregular but i heard that zinc will help is that true?** 14 year old girl.

Dear 'Coming on worrier' – Girls' periods normally start any time between 10 years old and 16 years old, so the fact that you haven't started yet is perfectly normal. Taking zinc will make no difference at all. The hormones in your body will start you off when they are ready. If you look on the positive side – think of all the money you will save on sanitary pads and/or tampons.

Dear Doctor Ann – **I think I'm getting my period. How do I tell mum and should I wear a tampon or pad?**

Dear 'Think I am starting my periods' – Yes, do tell your mum. She is going to be your best friend for things like this, even though you may feel a bit embarrassed to tell her.

Remember, she will also have started her periods at about your age and is likely to still be having them. If you are worried that your period might start when you are out or at school, it is a good idea to wear a small panty liner. If you tell your mum, she will probably buy them for you.

Dear Dr Ann – **Is it normal for a girl age 10 to grow pubic hair and underarm hair? I sweat a lot, too.** 10 year old girl.

Dear 'Worried about pubic and underarm hair growth and sweating' – Yes, it is normal for some 10-year-olds. The hormones that cause all these changes may start to kick in when you are 10, or even sometimes earlier. As well as all the things you usually associate with puberty, like breasts, getting taller, periods, and pubic hair, the hormones also affect sweat glands and some special glands called apocrine glands. Our bodies are covered in sweat glands: 3–4 million of them. Certain parts of our body, like our armpits, have lots of them. The apocrine glands are also in our armpits, and they produce some chemical stuff which give us our body odour (smell). Deodorants can help stop the sweating and the smell.

Dear Dr Ann – **If I have ginger hair will I have ginger pubic hair when I get older?** 11 year old girl.

Dear 'Will I have ginger pubic hair' – Yes, you probably will have ginger pubic hair if all your other hair is ginger.

● 8–11 years:	no outside signs yet, but the hormones are starting to work
● 8–14 (average 11–12) years:	starting to grow a little. Growth can stop and start.
● 9–15 (average 12–13) years:	continue to grow, but shapes can vary enormously
● 10–16 (average 13–14) years:	get fuller and rounder till they are almost adult shape
● 12–19 (average 15) years:	adult shape

Dear Dr Ann – **I am 14 nearly 15 and i haven't got n e boobs.**
Everyone takes the micky out of me and once wen i woz playing
football i was tackling a boy and his brother said that he should be
the girl and i should be the boy. I haven't started my period yet but
wen i do does that mean that i will develop breasts. Is it true that u
grow up 2 b the same chest size as your mum? 14 year old girl.

Dear 'Haven't got n e boobs yet' – As far as your boobs
are concerned, stop worrying, they will start to grow and your
periods will start. Lots of 14-year-olds are in your position. Give
your body and hormones a chance and it will all start up soon.
You may end up the same size as your mum was at your age but
it's not always like that. Boys love teasing girls (and sometimes
vice versa). The best way to deal with teasers is either to tease
them back or ignore them.

Dear Doctor Ann – **I've got big boobs – sizes B32 to C30 and I
am worried I will never start my periods.** All my mates have started.
12 year old girl.

Dear 'Size B32' – Stop worrying. Most, but not all, girls get their breasts before they get their periods – so you are one of the crowd. Chill out, give your body time and your periods will happen all too soon.

● CHANGES IN SHAPE, HEIGHT AND FIGURE

● *8–11 years:*	*no changes visible*
● *8–14 (average 11–12) years:*	*may start to get a lot taller and put on weight (or in some cases, lose it)*
● *9–15 (average 12–13) years:*	*body still growing, and shape changes can be dramatic*
● *10–16 (average 13–14) years:*	*underarm and leg hairs appear*
● *12–19 (average 15) years:*	*usually fully grown with adult figure by this stage*

● HOW DO YOU FEEL?

Dear Dr Ann – **do people get moody all the time when they are going through puberty?** 13 year old girl.

Dear 'Does puberty make you moody' – Lots of girls and boys do find they are more moody than they have been in the past when they start to go through puberty. Sometimes these sudden mood swings make you feel great one moment, and cross, tearful, or depressed the next. Once again, it seems to be because of those hormones that whizz around your body. But not everyone gets moody, and if you really feel moody and depressed all the time, you might need some help. Otherwise, realize that the bad mood will soon pass and you'll feel back on top again.

4 Penises

size, shape and those odd spots

It is just as well that boys do not spend too much time displaying their willies in public, because if there is one part of their body that they are obsessed with – it is usually their willy. Is it long enough, straight enough, spotless and totally perfect (in the eyes of the owner and any girl lucky enough to see it)? As boys don't go around (most of the time) in a state of nakedness, the only chance of comparing their willy with others tends to be in the showers at school.

● SIZE

The main thing that most boys worry about is whether their penis is a normal size or not. They are in luck because an American doctor did some research and measured thousands of boys' penises and found that the normal floppy size for:

- 10-year-olds is 4–8 cm   (1.6–3.2 inches)
- 12-year-olds is 5–10 cm   (2–4 inches)
- 14-year-olds is 6–14 cm   (2.4–5.5 inches)
- 16-year-olds is 10–15 cm (4–5.9 inches)
- 18-year-olds is 11–17 cm (4.3–6.7 inches)

However, he also found that however small the floppy size is, over 90% of men's penises grow to around 14 to 18 cm when erect.

Dear Doctor Ann – Well I'm 15 years old and I have a 5.5 inch penis but I'm wondering where to measure my penis from – I think that's something that most people ignore.

Dear 'Penis measurer' – Penis measurements are usually taken on men's penises when they are NOT erect. The measurement is taken from the base of your penis on its top side below your tummy to the tip of the penis, but without stretching your penis! I hope this is understandable and good luck.

Dear Doctor Ann – When I was in a P.E. lesson in Year 8, we were offered to take a shower. I did not need one because I did not do much in that lesson but most of the boys did. But they always want to look at each others dicks? Why do they do this?

Dear 'Curious about dick viewing' – Boys tend to look at one another's penises, when they get the chance, in order to check out how the size and shape of other boys' equipment compares with their own – not usually because they fancy one another. It's just curiosity.

Dear Dr Ann – **Does smoking weed decrease the size of your penis?** 16 male.

> *Dear 'Weed wonderer' –* There's no evidence that smoking weed makes your penis smaller, or bigger for that matter, though some guys complain that it makes it more difficult to get an erection.

● HOW IT HANGS

Hi Dr Ann – **OK I'm a 14-year-old male with an average size penis BUT it curves.** Also I can masturbate fine but its only like 5 pumps and I'm done. Could it be because my penis curves down and to the left or could it be a more serious problem? And also the curve I CAN'T GET IT STRAIGHT and it scares me what my g/f mite think of me. 14 year old boy.

> *Dear 'Male with curved penis' –* You are completely normal. Boys' penises can curve to the left and curve to the right and curve down a bit, and when erect can even curve up a bit – all just the way nature made you boys. You say that when you masturbate, it is five pumps and you're done. If you want to last longer, then take it slower and try and think of non-sexy things so as to delay things. None of what you say in your question need worry you.

● YOUR KNOB ENDS

The glans is the smooth end to your penis under the foreskin (unless it has been circumcised). The foreskin is the loose bit of skin at the end of boys' penises that normally covers the glans (or bell end) of the penis. All boys are born with this loose bit of skin at the end of their penises. In some boys it is possible to pull this bit of skin right back over the bell-shaped end of the penis; in others, it is not. It is the foreskin that is removed when a boy is circumcised.

Dear Dr Ann – just under my 'bell end' there is a big purple ring – is this normal?

Dear 'Purple-ringed bell end owner' – Yes, the bell end or knob of your penis is officially known as the glans (this is the normal medical term). It is very sensitive, which is why you have a foreskin to protect it. If you can pull your foreskin right back (and many boys can't which is also OK), then you may notice a darker purple ring around the base of your glans. This is more obvious in some boys than others, but is nothing to worry about.

Dear Doctor Ann – I can't seem to pull my foreskin over the whole of my knob end even when I'm floppy – is this normal?

Dear 'Have I got a normal foreskin?' – Yes, it sounds as though your foreskin is quite OK. Don't try pulling and forcing it right back if it won't go easily, as it can get stuck and get sore and swollen. If you have no trouble peeing, there is nothing to worry about.

The average penis comes in as many colours as there are skin colours of people in the world. Penises also come with a considerable variety of normal lumps and bumps on them.

Doc – **I am 14, and I have this brown mark down the underside of my penis.** It looks like a really large vein, but it doesn't feel like one. What should I do?

Dear 'Person with brown mark on penis' – Many men have a line on the underside of their penis which is browner than the rest of the skin of their penis. This line is usually fairly straight and stretches all along the middle of the underside of their penis. I am afraid that I haven't been able to find any particular reason for this – it is not always clear why there is so much variation in your average humans, but it helps make us the individuals we are.

Dear Doctor Ann – **I have what looks like a type of a whitehead zit on my penis. What could it be?** 15 year old boy.

Dear 'Person with white zits on his penis' – You have something in common with probably every other boy/man on the planet. Penises usually come with small round lumps, about 1 mm across, which are usually to be found around the base of your penis and the underside. These are

normal 'glands', some of which will, if you squeeze them (not recommended but not particularly harmful!), produce a kind of white cheesy substance. Some, at the base of your penis, may also have hairs growing out of them.

Hi Dr Ann — **I have never had any sexual activities but I have got yellow spots at the base of my penis head.** It does not hurt or give me any problems. I think it has been there for about 3 years. Is this a problem? 16 year old boy.

> *Dear 'Yellow spots worrier'* – Cease to worry. Your standard male penis comes with a whole assortment of bumps and lumps, and your 'yellow bumps' sound to me to fit in with these. Though I am not absolutely sure what causes the yellow bumps, I can tell you that they are usually found on the underneath of your 'tip' or 'bell end' or 'glans', along the 'frenulum' – the bit of skin that attaches your foreskin to the underside of your glans. They are usually there for a long time, but may also come and go. You absolutely don't have some terrible disease!

Dear Doctor Ann — **I have recently experienced a problem of which the symptoms are small hard lumps (1 mm in diameter) all over my dick!!** These have remained for about a year and are not painful. They are easier to see when I have a hard on. 15 year old boy.

> *Dear 'Lumpy penis'* – I think that it would be an extremely useful thing if I could put up some photos of boys' penises on my website, but I doubt whether the powers that be would allow it – even if it would set millions of boys' minds at rest.

What you describe are absolutely normal and occur on most boys'/mens' penises. They occur mainly around the base of the penis and on the underside – but you may also find some along other parts of your shaft. They are around 1 mm in diameter, usually quite soft, and sometimes they may secrete a whitish/yellow substance. They are normal skin glands and you can stop worrying about them.

● THE 'SMELLY' WILLY PROBLEM

Dear Dr Ann – **what shall I do – my boyfriend has a very smelly willie?** 15 year old girl.

Dear 'Girl whose boyfriend has a very smelly willy' – The simple answer is: don't go near him/it until he has washed. Some people (as you have discovered) produce more smell than others (just like some are tall and some are short). Those that produce more smell need to wash more often, and it sounds as if your boyfriend either doesn't wash himself often enough (and this may need to be several times a day) or doesn't wash his underclothes often enough. Deodorants may help, but basically thorough washing with soap and water has served for hundreds, if not thousands, of years and will continue to do so. It is *his* responsibility and you should tell him so. If he doesn't take action – dump him.

5 Penises
ups, downs and roundabouts

HOW ERECTIONS HAPPEN

The inside of the penis contains small cavities like a sponge. When boys get an erection, the blood flow out of the penis is cut down by a valve, but the blood flowing in keeps going and all those cavities fill with blood. Similar kinds of changes occur in a woman's clitoris when she is sexually excited, though of course a clitoris is much, much smaller than a penis.

● STIFFIES, BONIES, HARD-ONS...

Dr Ann – **when I get an erection my penis sticks straight up. Is this normal?** 14 year old boy.

Dear 'Boy with a penis that sticks straight up' – Some boys' penises, when erect, will stick straight upwards, others straight out, others somewhat down. They may also stick out a bit to the left or a bit to the right – but actually upwards is the commonest direction! No problems with any of these – just human variation.

Dear Doctor Ann – **every time i kiss a girl i always get a stiffy** and its annoying cause if we hug together when we're kissing then well you know she can feel it and i

have to back off so we end up being really nervous around each other p.s. please help. 15 year old boy.

Dear 'Gets a stiffy when kissing a girl' – I am afraid that there is no easy way to cure this. What is happening to you and your penis is an entirely straightforward reaction when you get sexually excited. You can (a) try not to kiss your girlfriend; (b) try thinking of something like the contents of your refrigerator while your are kissing your girlfriend so as not to get too excited; (c) reassure your girlfriend that what is happening to your penis is normal, and explain that it doesn't necessarily mean that you want to go any further.

Dear Doctor Ann – **I get erections looking at men is that OK?** 15 year old male.

Dear 'Gets erections looking at men' – That is perfectly OK. You may be asking this question because you are worried about being gay, but there is no need to worry about it. If it does turn out that you are attracted to men more than women, then so be it. However, your sexual feelings may not be fully developed, so be patient and see what kind of relationships you develop in the future – no need to get too worked up about it now!

Dear Doctor Ann – **I wake up with a bony every morning.** I'm embarrassed that my mum will see it, what shall I do? 14 year boy.

Dear 'Morning bony getter' – Your morning erection (which almost all boys/men seem to get at one time or another) is your body just making sure that the system that gives you your erections is working OK. I can entirely understand that it is embarrassing to have your mother come in when you are lying there in your erect state, but you can always lie on your side or, if it is not too painful, on your tummy, and politely ask your mother to leave the room while you get up.

Dear Doctor Ann – **my penis sticks straight out even when flaccid.** When I wear jeans it looks like I have a very small hard-on. Is there anything I can do? 16 year old boy.

Dear 'Permanent small hard-on person' – When boys' penises are in their 'flaccid' state, some are more flaccid than others. Some boys' penises are completely flaccid and appear to be really quite small till they get a hard-on; other boys' penises are permanently in a semi-hard state – it is all part of standard human variation and actually gives no indication of the size of a man's penis when he has a full erection. I do quite understand that it must be rather difficult trying to disguise the lump which your penis makes in your trousers, particularly if they are tight. You can try wearing 'containing' Y-fronts, or buy jeans which are somewhat looser fitting. Some boys, instead of letting their penis hang down, actually have it in their pants pointing straight up, which may make it less obvious.

Dear Doctor Ann – **I can pull my foreskin when it's hard but my erection is so strong that it appears that my foreskin will tear apart & its really painful.** What should i do. Also if I touch the head of my penis it is very very painful. plz help. 16 year old boy.

Dear 'Person with painful erection' – What you should do about this depends on whether you pull your foreskin right back before you have an erection or not. If you pull your foreskin right back before you get an erection, then you can solve the problem by not pulling your foreskin right back over the whole bell end of your penis, but just a little bit back. If, however, you are getting a great deal of pain from your foreskin and it is not pulled back, then your foreskin is so tight that you ought to go and see a doctor about it.

● **SMEGMA OR KNOB CHEESE**

This is the greasy white stuff that boys get under their foreskin. It is entirely normal and is mainly made up of dead skin cells of the glans (bell end) of the penis.

Dear Doctor Ann – I know that you're really busy and all that – but I would really appreciate it if you could tell me what is the matter with my 'cock' – can I use that word? Anyway I keep finding skin that has come off on my bell end, and I don't know what's causing it to happen, its not painful but it seems that there's lots of it coming off... can you help me please? 15 year old boy.

Dear 'Skin off the cock sufferer' – Don't worry – almost all men who are uncircumcised get a greasy substance called 'smegma' under their foreskin. You are probably right that there are some dead skin cells in the stuff you are finding (dead skin cells come off all parts of your body all the time – like when your skin gets flaky or your head gets dandruff). But the stuff on your 'bell end' is mainly greasy secretions from normal glands in the skin folds at the end of your penis. All you need to do is to pull the skin back off your 'bell end' and gently wash the stuff off.

Dear Ann – **my penis often emits an unpleasant fishy smell especially when erect.** Is this normal? If not what is it and how do I stop it? 15 year old boy.

Dear 'Person with a fishy smell' – This smell is probably due to normal cells that come off your penis head (bell end, or glans) and get stuck under your foreskin. These cells produce 'knob cheese' or 'smegma', which is the white stuff that you may find under your foreskin. The smell usually becomes more obvious when you get an erection, because your foreskin gets pulled back and this allows the smell out. You can easily stop the smell from happening just by washing your 'bell end' more frequently. If you can, when you have a bath, or even between having a bath, gently pull your foreskin right back over your 'bell end' and wash around it with soap and warm water – that is all that is needed.

WHERE DID YOUR FORESKIN GO?

Circumcision is the operation carried out on the penis of some boys, which involves removing the piece of skin that covers the tip of the penis, called the 'foreskin'. It is most commonly removed at birth for religious reasons. It is possible that originally it was done for reasons of cleanliness. The main medical reason for a boy/man having to be circumcised is if the hole in the foreskin at the end of their penis is so tight that when they pee, the foreskin balloons out. When someone needs a circumcision for this reason, an anaesthetic is always used!

Dear Doctor Ann – **I have been circumcised and am worrying how it will affect me with girls.** 13 male.

Dear 'Worried about being circumcised' – Don't worry about this. Most boys who are circumcised have it done as a baby for religious reasons. In fact, nearly half the men in the world have probably been circumcised and it doesn't seem to affect their sex lives with girls at all.

Dear Dr Ann – **Please could you tell me what a circumcised penis looks like?** I have no reason that I know of to be circumcised but from what i've read i'm unsure as to whether i have been. I have a thin red line on the underside of my penis (visible when erect) although i still have what i think to be loose skin. I am also unable to pull my foreskin down to expose my penis head. Please help me. i'm very confused. 14 year old boy.

Dear 'Wanting to know what a circumcised penis looks like' – Put simply, someone who has been circumcised has had the loose bit of skin which normally covers the glans or 'bell end' of their penis removed, so that their bell end – the smooth purple end – of their penis is fully exposed. However, not all people who remove this bit of skin are as good at doing it as others, and therefore some remove more skin and some remove less skin. The thin red line on the underside of your penis may just be your 'frenulum', which is a bit of skin on the underside of your glans. Even in boys who have not been circumcised, their foreskin may get pulled back a bit off their glans when they are erect. It clearly sounds as if you have not been circumcised. Even when people have a foreskin, they cannot always pull it right back over their bell end. This should not worry you and is perfectly normal.

6 Boys' balls
and what 'comes' out

A boy's two balls/testes drop down into their 'ball bag' or 'scrotum' at puberty. Their testes (as you may have already discovered!) are extremely sensitive, but they hang in their sac on the outside of their bodies to help keep them cool, as they operate best at producing sperm at a lower temperature than you normally find inside the body. The adult testicle is about the size of a large elongated marble. Quite often they are slightly unequal in size and hang at slightly different levels within their ball bag.

Dear Dr Ann – **I have an ache in my balls** & i dont know what to do pppllleeeaaassseee help...? It happens when I get all sexed up. 15 year old boy.

> *Dear 'All sexed up person with painful balls' –* No one can explain exactly why this happens, but it is common. What seems to

occur is that if a boy gets sexually excited and doesn't then have an orgasm or 'come', he may get very painful balls or a strong ache in the groin. The pain will go away within a few minutes or so (usually up to a quarter of an hour). Sometimes boys find that if they give themselves an actual orgasm by masturbating, then the pain does go. However, other boys find they actually get 'ball ache' after they have 'come'.

Dear Doctor Ann – **I quite often get a really bad ache in my right testicle – what is it?** 14 year old boy.

Dear 'Aching right testicle owner' – Although it is very common to get aching balls, especially when one gets sexually aroused, if the ache is only in one of your testicles, you should have it checked out by a doctor.

Dear Doctor Ann – **I have a lump on my groin area.** What does this mean? i have been kicked numerous times in the testicle region and i was wondering if this prevents production of sperm. (live sperm?). 16 year old boy.

Dear 'Lump in the groin person' – I'm sorry to hear you have had numerous kicks in the balls, but it should not prevent you making sperm. I'm afraid I can't tell what this lump in your groin is without seeing or feeling it. It may be a lymph gland, which can swell up for various reasons, or even a hernia. Sometimes a lump in the groin means that one of your balls hasn't descended into your ball sac (scrotum), and you can check this out by making sure that you have two testes in your ball bag. All funny lumps in this area should get checked out by a doctor.

Dear Doctor Ann – **if I get punched in the balls will it stop me from producing sperm again?**

Dear 'Sperm producer' – The main problem with getting punched balls is just how incredibly painful it is (as you may have already discovered!). Sometimes, after being kicked or punched in the balls, they may become swollen, bruised and feel very tender. This may last for a few days. Wearing Y-fronts will give support and will help the tenderness. As for not being able to produce sperm and have children, the answer is that you certainly can – so don't use it as a method of contraception! Almost all men get bashed in the balls sometime in their life, so if it stopped sperm production, there wouldn't be any babies around!

Dear Dr Ann – **i have got one testicle that is far larger than the other.** One is pea sized the other is far larger – about the size of a brussels sprout. Help me please! 15 year old boy.

Dear 'Big and little testis owner' – The size difference of your testes sounds a bit abnormal as a testis should not be pea-sized. Please go and get them checked by your doctor and don't be embarrassed.

Dear Dr Ann – **my ball bag keep itchin. Is that a problem?** Age: 12. Sex: male.

Dear 'Itchy ball bag owner' – It is obviously a problem for you as it is uncomfortable. The most likely reason is

that you are wearing pants made of nylon or other material that makes you sweaty and your skin very hot and itchy. Try wearing loose *cotton* boxer shorts and see if this helps. Sometimes, the skin covering your balls gets a fungal infection, rather like athletes foot between your toes, and this can also itch. Other causes include a skin problem called eczema, which can make your skin dry and flaky. All these things can easily be sorted with different creams available from the doctor or the chemist.

Dear Doc – **my ball bag is sometimes all smooth and other times all crinkly – is this normal?** 14 year old boy.

Dear 'Smooth and crinkly ball bag owner' – I think that you might find that when your balls hang low (usually when the weather is hot or you have had a hot bath), then your ball bag (scrotum) will be relaxed and your balls hang low and the skin on the outside will be fairly smooth. When it gets cold or you have been swimming in cold water, then your ball bag crinkles up due to a muscle in its wall, called the cremaster muscle, contracting. This is all to keep your testes at the right temperature for them to produce sperm.

● SPERM

Dear Doctor Ann – **what is 'cum'?** 15 year old girl.

Dear 'Curious about cum' – 'Cum' can also be spelt 'come' and is what boys produce when they have an orgasm and ejaculate. A boy's normal 'cum' is a thick, yellowish fluid – about a teaspoonful – which contains his 'sperms', and is also made up of water, sugar and proteins. If you don't want to get pregnant when a boy 'comes' inside your vagina, then you must use some form of contraception.

Fascinating facts about sperm

- Immature sperm are present in baby boys but need the puberty hormone surge to make them grow into big sperm.
- About 2–6 ccs (about a teaspoonful) of fluid is ejaculated each time a man 'comes'.
- The sperm itself only makes up about 5% of what a man ejaculates.
- These 2–6 ccs contain around 100 million sperm, plus a mixture of sugar, protein, Vitamin C, zinc and prostaglandins (which help the sperm on their travels).
- When sperm is ejaculated, it is like a gel which liquefies in about 5–15 minutes. Only when this gel becomes liquid do the sperm really get going – about 30 minutes later (but it may take up to 24 hours).
- It only takes one sperm to get a woman pregnant!
- Sperm can hang around for a long time inside a woman – up to four days or more.

Dear Doctor Ann – **what is human sperm made up of?**

Dear 'Curious about human sperm' – Each sperm is made up of three parts – the head, the middle and the tail. Think of it like a missile ready to launch. The head is the missile's warhead and contains the genetic material (chromosomes). When the sperm meets up with the woman's egg (ovum), the two join up and the egg is fertilized. The middle bit of the sperm is very complicated and controls the sperm's activities. The tail is like a propeller and speeds the sperm to its target – the egg. However, the sperm (spermatozoa) themselves make up only about 5% of what a man ejaculates each time he comes, even though there are around 100 million of them! So they are very, very, very tiny. The rest of what a man ejaculates in his 'come' or 'ejaculate' is a mixture of lots of other substances to help support the sperm on its journey to meet the woman's egg.

Dear Doctor Ann – **my sperm is not white. It has some lumps and grey patches in it. Is that normal?** 15 year old boy.

Dear 'Sperm worrier' – The sperm which you ejaculate is made up of a whole lot of different things. Only 5% of what comes out when you ejaculate is actually the sperm itself. The rest is made up of water, sugar, protein, and a whole lot of other things. Sometimes 'come' looks very thin and grey (especially if you have been masturbating rather a lot, so you won't have so many sperm in your come). Sometimes 'come' can look thick, yellow and lumpy. All this variation is entirely normal... so relax.

Dear Doctor Ann – **is it possible to run out of fertile sperm if you masturbate a lot?** 16 year old boy.

Dear 'Running out of fertile sperm' – No, you don't 'run out of sperm', but what comes out when you ejaculate may become thinner and contain less actual sperm if you masturbate very frequently. But this is only very temporary and within a few hours or a day, your sperm count will be back up again.

QUIZ 1 HOW SEXWISE ARE YOU?

1
The sexiest bit of you is:
- a   your brain
- b   between your legs
- c   your outstanding looks

2
If you fancy someone, do you:
- a   immediately text message them 'I want 2 do text with u'?
- b   feel totally shy and do nothing?
- c   find some way of talking to them and see if you have something that you both like doing together?

3
During a boy's puberty:
- a   he should grow as hairy as a gorilla
- b   his balls (testes) should grow in size about 7 times
- c   no black curly pubic hair by 12 means he should go and see his doc

4
During a girl's puberty:
- a   she should get boobs as big as melons before she is 16
- b   a white vaginal discharge means she's got a sex infection
- c   on average she starts her changes before boys

5
Boys' willies:
- a   hang straight down – unless excited
- b   can get a stiffy even when their owners are not thinking of Britney naked
- c   can smell worse than a 10-day-old dead fish unless washed regularly

If you got them all right – then you are sexwise.

If you got them all wrong – then stay away from the opposite sex!

Answers

1 **a** (though you may think otherwise!)

2 **c** (well, it's worth a try!)

3 **b** (but if you're a boy don't boast about it, and if a girl don't immediately ask to see them)

4 **c** (which is why most of the girls in your class are taller than the boys)

5 **b and c** (so boys should wash their knobs and girls should stay away from boys who don't wash their knobs).

Boobs

7 and breasts

Breasts are made up of fat, muscle, milk ducts and glands. They come in all shapes and sizes. Breasts develop during early puberty, usually before girls' periods start, but after they get pubic hairs. Breasts can feel rather like lumpy porridge, but tend to get a bit tender and a bit lumpier just before periods because of the effects of hormones circulating around in the blood.

The nipple and areola (the darker circle around the nipple) vary in size from person to person and are sensitive to touch! Touching them can be sexually arousing and can make the nipples become more erect and stick out more. Although they do play a big part in sex, breasts are also there to produce milk for a baby when it is born.

Dear Doctor Ann – **I'm 15 and I hate my breasts – they are like tiny dots on the face of my chest, what can I do?**

Dear 'Girl with dots' – You haven't stopped growing yet at 15, and your breasts will probably grow bigger if you wait a bit. Don't judge what size you should be by what appear as breasts on models in films, underwear adverts, magazines, music videos, etc. These breasts have often been taped, surgically enhanced, digitally altered, pushed up, pushed down, pushed out, pushed in – all in the name of artificial perfection.

Dear Doctor – **i was just wanting to know whether breast size really matters when having sex?** Or is it just that men like women with big breasts? Thanks. 16-year-old girl.

Dear 'Curious about the effect of breast size on sex' – The size of breasts does not make any difference when having sex itself. Girls are often unhappy with the size of their breasts (as boys are with their penises). You have breasts in order to feed your babies when they are born (if you choose to have them), but, but, but – yes, they do also attract the attention of boys. Boys' answers, when asked what size of breast they like best on girls, vary hugely. Some like large breasts. Some like medium breasts. Some like small breasts. Most of all, they like the whole girl who has the breasts. It is her personality and how she is as a whole that matters. Don't tell me that you would choose a boy just from the size and shape of his penis!!!

Dear Ann – **is there any way to make my boobs bigger?** I haven't really got breasts, I've got a pair of fried eggs stuck to my lungs. Girl aged 15.

Dear 'Wanting to make your breasts bigger' – Ask any woman about their breasts and almost all will, at one time or another, want to change them just a little bit. But if women were able to see the huge normal variation that exists in real women's breast sizes and shapes, then maybe they would change their minds and accept what they have got. Most doctors won't even consider operating on girls under the age of 18 – thank goodness – unless there are extremely good medical reasons. The breast owner's perception of 'beauty' isn't normally one of them! Before considering surgery, even if you are over 18 years old, you should look at all the other options: wearing different bras, having your bras enhanced or changed, counselling, psychological advice, etc.

Dear Ann – This is really winding me up so i was wondering if u could perhaps answer my question. **I've just turned 14 but my breasts are 32F. I told my best friend and her cousin overheard – now its all round the school! Am I normal?!** I'm only a size 10–12 and no one in my family is large, so what's going on? Will they get smaller and if they continue to grow, will i need a breast reduction??? plzzz answer this… Girl aged 14.

Dear 'Person worrying about too big breasts' – Stop getting wound up – you are NORMAL, NORMAL, NORMAL. I can't predict what size or cup shape you will finally be. Meanwhile, make sure you have a bra that fits well so as to feel comfortable. Fortunately, we are all different in size and shape and you are very likely to be different from your best friend or her cousin. It sounds like you need to talk to your best friend's cousin about keeping secrets. As for the whole school knowing (perhaps you are exaggerating a little bit?) – I doubt that anyone who is worth anything is going to like you more or less because they know what bra size you are!

Doctor Ann – **why are my sister's tits bigger than mine?** There has to be another reason other than the fact that she is older than me. Girl age 10.

Dear 'Girl age 10 with smaller tits than sister' – Most girls of 10 will not have grown tits yet because they will not have gone through puberty. The fact that your sister is older is probably the only reason for hers being bigger. But remember, everyone is different, even in one family, with some sisters having bigger tits than others. Breast growth stops later than people think – even into your 20s or 30s, though the major part of breast growth does occur between 10 and 18 years of age.

Dear Dr Ann – **Can the contraceptive pill make your breasts grow?** And if so, which type do make them grow? Girl aged 16.

Dear 'Does the pill make your breasts grow' – Many girls, but not all, find that taking the pill makes their breasts bigger. There are lots of different brands of contraceptive pills, which contain different types and quantities of the hormones oestrogen and progesterone. There is no one type that makes your breasts grow, but some types do seem to affect different women's breasts in a variety of ways. However, it's probably not a good idea to take the pill *just* to make your breasts bigger because of the side effects that may occur when taking the pill.

● DIFFERENT SHAPES AND OTHER WORRIES

Dear Dr Ann – **Why are my breasts so far apart?** One points left and the other right, my nipples stick out and I have no cleavage at all. I hate being able to see my toes. Girl aged 14.

Dear 'Worried about breasts and nipples' – Some women have breasts that are far apart, and for others they are close together. Similarly, nipples and their surroundings can vary from being the size of a 5p piece up to the size of a 50p piece. Nipples may stick out, be flat, or even inverted so that the centre of the nipple sticks inwards.

Dear Ann – **I don't know what my bra size is, I'm too embarrassed to go to a bra shop and ask...** pliz help. 14-year-old girl.

Dear 'Bra size measurer' – Get a tape measure and measure around your chest under your breasts, where your bra strap goes, and then add 5 inches to that measurement. Next, measure around your breasts and chest at the level of your nipples. The two numbers may be approximately the same or different. If they are roughly the same, then you need an AA-cup. If there is around a one inch difference, then you need an A-cup; if the difference is two inches, then a B-cup; and three inches would be a D-cup. When you have done this, buy the bra size which you think is right for you in a store that will 'exchange' – so that you can always take it back.

Dear Doc – **I am on my period and my nipples have bumps all over them** and the part that sticks out has changed – is this normal? They almost look like oddly shaped zits! Thanks. Age: 17 girl.

> *Dear 'Person with funny bumps on her nipples'* – I think it is the hormone changes that happen during the month and around your period that are making your nipples bumpy and sticking out more than normal. You will also probably notice that your breasts themselves are slightly bigger and lumpier before your period than at other times of the month. Why not keep a check on what happens during next month.

● **AND WHAT SOME BOYS THINK...**

Dr Ann – **Don't you find it disgusting that boys of my age blab on about how girls must have breasts the size of a football to be sexy.** I think it is crap. I like girls who don't try to make their breasts bigger with padded bras or vice versa whether they be big or small. Why do those weirdos think like that? Boy aged 16.

> *Dear 'Boy who likes girls as they are'* – I am sure that the girls who read this will be really pleased that you want girls to feel good about their breasts whatever they are like. I'm not sure why some boys and men are so obsessed with wanting girls to have big breasts. Certainly the media makes a lot of it all.

Girls' bits

what is there 'down below'

VAGINA, CLITORIS, ETC.

Contrary to what most girls and boys think, your biggest sex organ is your brain. But for girls there are also lots of other bits 'down there': vagina, ovaries, uterus, cervix, fallopian tubes, vulva, clitoris. Some of these are involved in sex itself, some in having a baby, and some in both.

● **THE VAGINA**

Dear Doctor Ann – **I'm not sure how many holes I have** and does your vaginal opening get wider when you start your period because mine seems to be very tight?! Or is this just because I'm very skinny because I do a lot of exercise??? Please help me: Girl age 13.

Dear 'Uncertain about number of holes' – All girls have three openings down below. The front one is your pee hole (urethra), the back opening is the poo hole (anus) where your body gets rid of waste faeces (turds, crap), and the middle one (a larger opening) is the vagina. The vagina is where the man's penis fits in during sexual intercourse, where the period blood comes out, and where the baby comes out when it is born. Don't worry that your vagina will be too narrow for the blood to come out when you start your periods. There will easily be enough room for this to happen. The vagina does change during puberty and it also gets wider when you are sexually stimulated and ready to have sex.

Dear Ann – **how big is a woman's vagina?** Age: 14. Sex: female.

Dear 'Person wondering about the size of the vagina' – The vagina is a tube about 7–10 cms (3–4 inches) long in an adult woman. It is smaller in girls but gets larger as they go through puberty. It leads from the neck of the womb, inside your body, to the vulva where it opens between your legs. The walls of the vagina are very stretchy and elastic, as you will feel if you use a tampon. It also stretches around a baby as the baby is born, or around the man's penis during sexual intercourse.

Dear Doctor Ann – **my vagina is covered with very dark thick awful hairs** that are really long so I used a hair removal cream on my bikini line and now there's a big rash with spots. Is this normal because the first time I used it there, there was no rash! Age: 13. Sex: female.

Dear 'Worried about hair down there' – I think you are talking about your vulva/labial lips rather than your vagina (which is the tube-shaped passage between your womb and the outside of your body). The vulva includes the vaginal opening, the clitoris and the labia – in fact all the area around the entrance to the vagina. It sounds as though your vulval skin is allergic to or irritated by the hair-removal cream, so look at the ingredients and try a different one next time.

Dear Dr Ann – **what is at the top of the vagina?** From girl aged 13.

Dear 'Wondering what is at the top of your vagina' – The vagina is like a tube, at the top of which is something called the cervix, which is the neck of the womb (uterus). The uterus is where the egg, if it gets fertilized, becomes embedded into the wall and grows into a baby. Between your ovaries and your uterus there are two thin tubes, one on either side, called the fallopian tubes. If you are not using contraception, the sperm swim up from the vagina, through the cervix, into the uterus and along the fallopian tubes and will, at certain times of the month, meet up with the egg that is drifting down after it has been released from the ovary. This is where fertilization occurs and the baby then starts to develop in the uterus.

● AT THE OUTSIDE OPENING TO THE VAGINA

Dear Doctor Ann – **I have weird bumps on my vulva.** I am a virgin so I don't think it is a sexually transmitted disease. I was wondering if it is normal to have bumps on the skin flaps. They are yellowish and I can only see them when I pull the skin back. Can you help me please? Age: 17. Sex: female.

Dear 'Weird bumps on your vulva' – I think that what you are seeing is perfectly normal. It is difficult to know exactly what the bumps are that you are describing without seeing them, but they are probably tiny glands present in the skin. If you are still worried, it might be a good idea to go and see your family doctor and ask her to check them out. She/he won't be embarrassed even if you might feel a bit shy, and she'll keep everything you tell her confidential.

Dear Dr Ann – OK – I'm so embarrassed about this and I don't know what to do. **My vagina is really messed up – the outer lips are normal but the inner ones are very big and loose.** I have a thing about the size of a thumbnail that is at the front and just kind of hangs there. Its kind of hard and feels funny. Am I even a girl? What's wrong with me? From scared girl age 14.

Dear 'Scared something is wrong with her vagina' – It does not sound as though you have anything physically wrong with you. Women vary enormously in the size of their vaginal lips – the outer lips are called the labia majora and are usually, but not always, bigger than the inner ones called the labia minora. We usually only know what we are like ourselves and don't have a chance to compare our own private parts with those of other people. However, if you are worried, do go and ask your doctor who will quickly be able to tell you if there is anything amiss.

Dear Doctor – **I am 13 and curious – what is my clitoris 4?**

Dear 'Curious about your clitoris' – In front of her urethra (pee tube) every girl has a clitoris. This is the female equivalent of a man's penis – the clitoris is there to give a girl pleasure, like the glans of a boy's penis! Like penises, clitorises come in different shapes and sizes, anything from a couple of millimetres to two or three centimetres. Only the front centimetre or so is uncovered when the small hood of skin that normally covers it is pulled back.

Dear Doctor Ann – **when we get erections, what is the girl's equivalent?** 14-year-old boy.

Dear 'Wonderer about erections in girls' – Girls have a clitoris, which is the equivalent of a boy's penis but much smaller. When a woman's clitoris is excited, it becomes full of blood and hardens up, rather like a man's penis, but it is still pretty small (although again, the actual size varies a lot from woman to woman). The clitoris is an incredibly sensitive organ, which is full of nerve endings. During sex, the penis pushes on the inner folds (labia) and these in turn stimulate the clitoris.

Girls' 'down below'

how those bits work

The body produces lots of different hormones.
These are chemical messengers which travel around
the body in the bloodstream. The female hormones
are called oestrogen and progesterone. The levels of
these hormones are controlled by the brain, and
change during the menstrual cycle. They also
stimulate the glands in the vagina and make them
produce a whitish fluid called a discharge. They can
also affect a girl's emotions.

• PERIODS

Doc – **periods are a real nuisance – so why do we have to have
them?** Girl aged 14.

Dear 'Periods are a nuisance' – The reasons for having
them is to prepare the lining of a woman's uterus (womb) for
the egg, if it has been fertilized by a sperm, to grow into a

baby. Every month a woman's brain sends special hormones to the ovaries so that an egg is released (ovulation). A short time after this, the hormone oestrogen causes the lining of the uterus (womb) to get thicker and become ready to receive the egg which travels down the fallopian tube to the uterus. If the egg does not get fertilized that month, the hormones give the signal that pregnancy is not going to happen and whoosh, out comes the egg, which is smaller than a pin head, in your next period, along with the cells and blood from the lining of the uterus that were not needed. But if you do get pregnant, the brain sends other hormones, including one called 'progesterone', so that you don't have a period, and the lining of the uterus stays all spongy and ready for the fertilized egg to attach itself and grow into a baby.

Dear Ann – **i forgot my period date i feel that it's been ages i have been moody.** girl age 16.

*Dear 'Forgot period date' –*It is very easy to forget exactly when your last period happened, especially if your periods are not very regular. Your moodiness might be because your period is due, especially if your breasts feel a bit tender too. Most girls notice some mood changes during the month as their period cycle happens, and some feel fed up and grumpy for a day or two just before the period itself. A small percentage of women get really bad Premenstrual Tension (PMT). Try jotting down the start of each period in your diary or ask your mum to keep a record, to help you know where you are in the month.

Dear Dr Ann – **I've been using tampons for a while now and have recently found that when I put 1 in it really hurts** at the bottom of my bladder and spine as if its pressing on something, I also suffer from heavy periods. Age 16 female.

Dear 'Tampon-troubled person' –
It's likely that you are using tampons
that are rather too large. Try smaller
ones or a different brand and see if
this helps.

Dr Ann – **whenever I try to put tampons in they don't hurt but when I get them in half way, I can't get it in any further** no matter which way i put it and I have read the instructions over and over again. is there something wrong with me? Aged 15 girl.

Dear 'Having problems with tampons' – Probably
there's nothing wrong with you and it can take a bit of practice
to put tampons in. You may be trying to push the tampon in at
the wrong angle or the tampon might be a bit too big.
Sometimes trying a thinner tampon helps, especially at the
beginning of a period when you may be a bit dry, as there
won't be much blood to lubricate the tampon and let it slip in
easily. Trying a different type of tampon with a different
applicator sometimes also helps. It may be that the hymen,
which is the thin skin covering the entrance to your vagina, is
a little thicker than in some people, or the hole in your hymen
which lets the blood out when you have a period is still very
small. Why not give it a rest for a few months. In the
meantime, use sanitary towels. Then after a while, try again.
There are several good little leaflets and books available about
all of this which you can get from a bookshop.

Doctor Ann – **can I swim when I have my period?** female aged 14.

> *Dear 'Can I swim when I have a period'* – There's no reason not to go swimming while you have your period, though unless you are using tampons, it is not hygienic for everyone else. Make sure you put in a new tampon before you go swimming.

● DISCHARGES

Hi – **I keep getting this white stuff in my knickers, and what is it?** Girl aged 12.

> *Dear 'Getting white stuff on your knickers'* – What you describe is a normal vaginal discharge that all girls and women get after puberty. It comes from the glands in your vagina, which become more active around puberty and produce mucus, which keeps the vagina comfortable. You may notice that there is a little more discharge just before you have a period – also due to the effect of hormones.

Doctor Ann – **I'm just curious as to what exactly is a normal discharge?** All the descriptions I've had have been pretty vague. I can get quite bad smelling discharge which sometimes looks as if it has a weird texture like jelly and it can range in colour from clear to white to a greeny-yellow colour. Is this normal and what exactly does the discharge look like when you have an infection? signed X a 15 year old girl.

Dear 'Curious about vaginal discharge' – Girls start to increase the amount of discharge they produce as they go through puberty and as the hormones start to work on the cells and glands in the vagina and neck of the womb. Before puberty, most girls have very little discharge. After puberty, what is normal for one girl will not be normal for another. Some will produce a lot of discharge, whilst others produce very little. Throughout the month you will also notice it varies in colour, how sticky it is and how much of it there is. What is not normal is if the discharge becomes smelly, itchy, or greenish in colour. Any of these may mean you have an infection, especially if you have put yourself at risk by having had sex without using a condom.

• THE SMEAR TEST

Dear Doctor Ann – **when do I have a smear test if I have done it without using protection.** Girl age 16.

Dear 'When should I have a cervical smear test' – Women, if they are sexually active, will need to start having cervical smear tests at the age of 20, and then they should have one every 3 years after this (unless there is some abnormality, when you might be advised to have a smear more frequently). The smear test involves the doctor or nurse inserting a special instrument into your vagina and scraping off some cells from the cervix (neck of your womb). These cells are then 'smeared' onto a glass slide and checked in the laboratory for any abnormalities, which can then be easily treated before they go on to develop into proper cancer. These abnormalities and cervical cancer are probably caused by a type of wart virus which is sexually transmitted. Condoms help protect you from catching this virus, as well as stopping you getting many other sexually transmitted infections.

Masturbation
a game for one or more hands

WHY PEOPLE DO IT AND HOW

People masturbate because...

- it is enjoyable
- it is easy
- it is controllable by yourself and you can find out what you like sexually
- it helps relieve feelings of sexual tension
- you do not get pregnant or get sexually transmitted diseases by doing it.

GOING IT ALONE

Dear Ann – **what is masturbation and can girls and boys do it?** Girl aged 15.

Dear 'Curious about masturbation' – Masturbation is the term normally used when either boys or girls sexually stimulate themselves. Boys usually do this by using their hand (or hands) to rub the skin of the shaft of their penis up and down. Girls normally do it by rubbing their clitoris, but may also masturbate by pushing their fingers in and out of their vaginas. So girls and boys can do it – not only to themselves, but also to each other. All this is entirely normal.

Dear Doc – **at what age should you start to masturbate?** Boy aged 13.

Dear 'What age to start masturbating' – There is no set age at which people start, and there is no 'should' about it – it is just if you want to! Sometimes, even very young children around one year of age find it gives them pleasure to play with themselves. It varies from person to person, and some boys and girls never masturbate and that's fine too.

Dear Doctor Ann – **my friend asked me the other day if I masturbated. I did not answer him and he made fun of me.** What should I do???? Boy aged 14.

Dear 'Person who doesn't want to answer' – Quite right too and don't feel embarrassed about whether you do or do not masturbate – because almost everyone does. Just tell your friend that it is none of his business. Whether you masturbate or not is entirely up to you and has nothing to do with your friends.

Dear Dr Ann – **other girls talk about 'cumming' by masturbating, how do you do it?** 15 year old girl.

Dear '15-year-old girl wanting to know about cumming' – I think that all that your friends are suggesting when they use the word 'cumming' for when girls masturbate, is that they are achieving orgasm. Orgasm is the feeling of having a peak of pleasure that people achieve during sex, after which people feel satisfied and don't want any more sex for a bit. People usually use the word to 'cum' or 'come' for either a boy or a girl when they actually have an orgasm, though the word might have originally only applied to boys making their sperm 'come' out of the end of their penis.

CAN YOU DO IT TOO MUCH?

Doc – **how often should you masturbate?** Boy 14.

Dear 'Person who wants to know how often' – There isn't really any right answer to this question. Some boys tell me that they masturbate four, six or even more times a day. Other boys write and say that they never masturbate. The ones who do it many times a day quite often worry that they will 'run out of sperm' – and although this may occasionally happen, it is only very temporary (a few hours or so). The limit to the amount that you masturbate is really connected to the problems of making you so exhausted you can't do anything else in life, and making yourself very sore from rubbing yourself all the time.

Dear Dr Ann – **I am 14 and I am afraid I masturbate too often.** I am afraid when I actually come to do the deed, it will not be as good and I will turn to masturbation again. I enjoy it greatly, but I am afraid what will happen if my parents catch me. Girl aged 15.

69

NO ENTRY

Dear 'Afraid I masturbate too often' – No, there really is no such thing as 'too often', unless you exhaust yourself or make yourself sore or do it in inappropriate places. I assume that you mean by 'come to do the deed' – having actual sexual intercourse. You should be waiting several years before experimenting with this (and even then, you will hopefully use contraceptives). But when you do, I think that with the right lover, you will find actual sexual intercourse no disappointment! I think that most young people worry about their parents or someone else catching them, but it only very rarely happens. Although it can be embarrassing, your parents will know all about what is happening and will hopefully be extremely discrete and just as anxious NOT to find you at it.

Dear Doctor Ann – **I have been masturbating for a while now and its starting to hurt! is this normal?** 14 year old boy.

Dear 'Hurting person' – This is a very common complaint – especially in boys who masturbate a lot. If you rub any bit of your skin enough, it will become sore as time passes (like your heel getting blisters when your shoes don't fit properly), and your penis is no exception. You might like to try using some 'lubrication' like KY jelly. You can buy it over the counter at your local chemist. Put it both on your knob end (glans) and the rest of your penis. If it continues to hurt, see your doctor and get it checked out in case there is something else causing the soreness.

Many boys and girls find that they enjoy the physical sensation of masturbating but not always how they feel immediately afterwards, as it may make them feel rather lonely and self-absorbed. Other girls and boys find that it gives them 'a sense of power', that it is 'liberating', 'gives them control'. Some have said that it is 'important because I don't have to be in a relationship to do it' and it 'taught me how to have an orgasm'. But people do also have worries about it...

Dear Ann – **hello i just want to ask a question about when i am masturbating, its all over in the next 3 minutes or so...** is this normal for a lad.???? 14 year old boy.

Dear '3-minute wonder person' – I am told by my male friends that there is huge variation in the time it takes boys to masturbate themselves to having an orgasm (or 'coming'). Some achieve it in less than a minute, and others may take as long as 10 minutes or more. All completely normal – so you can stop worrying.

Doctor Ann – **is it weird dat i cannot produce sperm?** I tried 2 masturbate a while ago and i couldn't and im afraid of trying again cos i might not b able 2. 14 year old boy.

71

Dear 'Person who cannot produce sperm' – Patience, patience. When boys begin to masturbate they don't always produce sperm. It may be that when you masturbate, you are not actually achieving 'orgasm', which means the point at which you ejaculate (spurt out) sperm. You will probably find that, with a bit of practice, you achieve the point where you do produce sperm. If not, and you are still worried, then try checking it out with your doctor.

Dear Doctor Ann – **does masturbation stunt the penis growth?** 13 year old boy.

Dear 'Worried about masturbation stunting penis growth' – I am not sure just how much actual research has been done on this. In the very short term masturbation undoubtedly makes your penis grow because you get an erection when masturbating. I am sure that it is fair to say that masturbation neither makes boys' penises grow bigger (other than making them have an erection) or smaller. Boys used to be told, many, many years ago, that if they masturbated, their penises would 'fall off'. Absolutely wrong again – if it was right, then most boys would not have penises!

Dear Dr Ann – **can masturbation cause weight gain??**

Dear 'Weight gain worrier' – Good question, but as far as I know, masturbation neither causes you to gain weight or to lose it. I can't think of any reason why it should cause you to gain weight, and I don't think that there is enough exercise involved to use up enough calories to cause you to lose weight!

Dear Doctor Ann – **can masturbating stop you from having children when you are older?** This is worrying me half to death. Please help. 15 year old boy.

> *Dear 'Worried that masturbating stops you from having children'* – There is absolutely no evidence that masturbation, either in boys or girls, does any harm whatsoever. Almost all boys, and many, many girls, masturbate and it has no effect at all on whether they can have babies later on in life.

Dear Doctor – **i'm very worried, im a girl and i masturbated by myself and now i'm not getting my period could i be pregnant?** Could someone have masturbated somewhere and left sperm there and i touched it and it somehow got on my hands and when i stuck my fingers in my vagina could it have gotten in?? im going crazy please help!

> *Dear 'Going crazy with worry'* – No, from what you tell me you can't be pregnant – so don't worry. When periods start, they may be irregular. Most people masturbate, so don't worry about that either.

● SO WHY ALL THE SECRECY?

Nowadays, many boys and girls are happy to admit, without a second thought, that they enjoy masturbating regularly. But for one reason or another (probably because of the way people considered masturbation in the past) some boys and girls do feel 'guilty', 'dirty', 'naughty' when they masturbate – **THERE IS ABSOLUTELY NO NEED TO...**

11 R U ready for sex?

NOT GOING THE WHOLE WAY

At around 13 or 14, some young people start sexual activities like kissing and touching one another, while others are not interested until they are older. Whatever your age, there are lots of sexy things that you can do with a partner, like snogging and touching, which do not involve actual sexual intercourse.

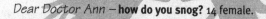

● **READY 4 SEX – BUT NOT 4 SEXUAL INTERCOURSE?**

Dear Doctor Ann – **how do you snog?** 14 female.

Dear 'Curious about snogging' – 'Snogging' is used as another word for 'kissing', and usually includes 'french kissing', where you put your tongue in the other person's mouth. It can also include hugging one another lying down or sitting up, and could also mean feeling parts of one another's bodies. Generally, it means getting very close to someone else without actually getting near to sexual intercourse, but probably different young people think differently in just how far you can go in a snog.

74

Dear Doc – **I've heard people talking about 'Touching up' girls, erm, please can you explain?** Boy age 15.

NO ENTRY

Dear 'Interested in touching up girls' – This means when boys go a bit further than snogging. It normally means that the boy touches parts of the girl's body like her breasts or her clitoris in order to get her 'sexed up' and excited. One reason boys enjoy doing this is because it gets them sexually excited too!

Hi Doctor – **my girlfriend lets me do 'heavy petting' to her,** for example, lets me stroke, rub, suck her breasts. I would think she would be a lot more restricted, and not let me do half as much as she lets me. Are women usually that open about their breasts? My girlfriend is a quiet person and has never done anything like this before. Boy aged 15.

Dear 'Heavy petter' – She may do this because she likes you and wants to give you pleasure, but also because she enjoys it. Why don't you talk to her about it – there isn't a right or wrong to this. Girls like having their breasts fondled as long as it's the right guy.

● R U READY 4 SEXUAL INTERCOURSE?

Sexual intercourse (where a man puts his penis into a girl's vagina) is illegal in the UK under the age of 16. In the United Kingdom, around three out of four women and two out of three men have *not* had sexual intercourse by the age of 16 – so you are in the in crowd if you are not doing it.

Dear Doctor – **Is it safe to have sex at my age??** 11 year old girl.

Dear 'Too young for sex' – **Absolutely NOT – NO, NO, NO** – it is dangerous, you could get pregnant and it is totally illegal at your age. Any girl who has sex at your age regrets it. Also, because it is totally illegal, whoever has sex with you could get prosecuted by the police.

Dear Dr Ann – **I am 15 years old and all my friends have had sex.** I'm the only one that has not. Should I have sex for this reason? 15 year old female.

Dear '15-year-old whose friends have all had sex' – This is certainly *not* a reason to have sex. I am sure that many of your friends have not had sexual intercourse yet. At 15, only one in four girls has had sex. By far the majority of girls have not had sex by the age of 16. It's you that's part of the crowd. Only have sex when you are in a loving relationship with someone you really trust and know. It is actually illegal to have sex under the age of 16, and many girls who have sex early regret it later.

Hi Doc Ann – **My girlfriend and I are both 12 and we would both like to have sex.** We are both mature enough to understand. What can we do? 12 year old boy.

76

Dear '12-year-olds who think they are mature enough to have sex' – I really think you are both kidding yourselves. You might think you are mature enough, but I am also sure that if you do go ahead and have sex, you will, in the future, realize that you weren't. There's PLENTY of time for sex and no need to rush into it. The other thing you need to know is that it is illegal to have sex under the age of 16 – but if you are determined to go ahead, please do go to a young person's clinic and talk it over, and *do* discuss contraception.

Hello Dr Ann – **Can you have sex if you haven't started your periods?** 14 year old girl.

Dear 'Can you have sex if your periods haven't started?' – Yes, you are able to have sexual intercourse before you have started your periods. But that does not mean that you should. If you are under the age of 16, then it is illegal for someone to have sex with you. What you also need to know is that you CAN GET PREGNANT, even if you haven't started your periods yet, because your eggs (ova) can start to get released from your ovaries even before you start your periods regularly. If you have sexual intercourse, your egg could get fertilized by the man's sperm.

Doctor Ann – **I am really worried about having sex because i wonder if it will hurt or not.** I really need some help. Also if I get my boyfriend to wear a condom then if i got him to wear 2 at once would I definitely not get pregnant. Please reply. Girl aged 16.

Dear 'Worried about having sex' – It sounds as if you may not be ready to have sex yet – so please don't go ahead if you have these sorts of worries. Sex does often hurt a bit, especially the first time, and particularly if you are tense and unsure if it is the right thing to be doing. As for guaranteeing that condoms will stop you getting pregnant, one condom used correctly should be OK, but sometimes things do go wrong. They do break or come off, especially if you are less experienced. But two condoms may cause more problems. If you do decide to go ahead, make sure your boyfriend (and you) know how to use the condom correctly. I think you should seriously think about waiting, and if any condom disaster happens – then go and get emergency contraception.

Dear Dr Ann – **I'm 17 and have a very loving boyfriend.** We're ready to have sex and are both virgins. I've read in a magazine that I'll bleed when I lose it – is this true and if so how much am i likely to bleed?

Dear 'Ready to lose it' – It sounds as if you have thought carefully about this – which is great. To answer your question: most girls, when they are virgins, do bleed when they first have intercourse, but the amount can vary from the odd drop of blood, to soaking a couple of sanitary towels. It's really never bad enough to need to see a doctor. If you have been using tampons, it is less likely to be so bad. Remember to use contraception.

12 When you don't want babies...

Contraception is any way of preventing a sperm from fertilizing a woman's egg to make a baby. If you are a teenager making love/having sexual intercourse with someone else and you are not using any contraception, you have a one in three chance of getting pregnant each time you have sex. If you have sex for a year without using contraception, then there is a 90% chance of the girl getting pregnant. If you are going to have sex – please, please make sure that you use contraception if you don't want to have a baby. You wouldn't cross a road if you were told that you had a one in three chance of getting killed – so why take the risk of getting pregnant! If you do *not* want to be a Daddy/Mummy just yet, there are at least 14 ways to stop it from happening. Some ways are better than others – crossing your fingers isn't one of them!

Dear Doctor Ann – **a boy I really trust and have liked for ages has asked me to have sex and I want to but I don't want to get pregnant** but I can't talk to my mum about it because she will just tell me not to! What shall I do? I need help! 16 year old girl.

Dear 'Wanting to have sex' – You sound as if you are taking a very sensible approach and I am just sorry that you can't talk to your mum, but I do quite understand. If you are actually starting on a long-term sexual relationship with your boyfriend, you need to know what all the contraceptive options are. In order to find out what all these are, you (and your boyfriend) can either go and see your local family doctor, or go to your local Family Planning Clinic or Brook Advisory Centre, and get them to tell you about the whole range of methods available – and then you can both decide together which is the best one for you both.

DON'T DO IT – ABSTINENCE MAKES THE HEART...

Dear Doctor Ann – **what can prevent me from getting pregnant.** 15 year old girl.

Dear 'Not wanting to get pregnant' – Luckily there are a great many things that you can do not to get pregnant. The first one is not having sexual intercourse. Think of all the other sexy things that you can do without actually doing IT. If you are going to have sexual intercourse, then the most obvious thing is to get the boy to wear a condom. This is very effective in stopping you both from having a baby and from getting some nasty sexually transmitted infection.

PUTTING UP THE BARRIERS

Barrier methods of contraception, like <u>condoms</u>, put something in the sperm's way and also help to stop you getting nasty bugs.

There are other barriers like the <u>cap/diaphragm</u>. These need to be fitted for size by a doctor or nurse and are put into the woman's vagina ahead of having sex. They should be used with some spermicidal cream to cover the cervix. These are not as safe as condoms, and some people think they are a bit messy.

Dear Dr Ann – **how does a condom work?** 13 female.

> *Dear 'How does a condom work' –* A condom is a bag made of thin rubber which fits tightly over a man's erect penis. If a man uses a condom during sexual intercourse, it catches the sperm when they come out as he ejaculates. The condom stops the man's sperm from joining with the woman's egg to make a baby. Condoms come in many different colours, tastes and types and can be obtained free from family planning clinics, young people's clinics and some GP surgeries. Otherwise, you can buy them from chemists, garages and in public toilets.

Dear Doctor Ann – **what do you do if a condom splits?**
Boy age 16.

Dear 'Condom splitter' – Take it seriously, talk to your girlfriend about it and don't pretend it didn't happen, or that it will be 'all right'. Next, get your girlfriend to get the 'emergency contraceptive pill' free from her doctor, or a young people's clinic, as soon as possible (but NOT in the middle of the night). Act as quickly as possible, because the best chance of stopping any pregnancy is to start taking the emergency contraceptive pill within 24 hours of the condom splitting. It usually acts well up to 3 days (72 hours) though. But if you haven't managed to get something done within three days, still see your doctor because they can help by inserting a 'coil' into your girlfriend's womb.

Dear Doctor Ann – **what is the percentage of teenagers getting pregnant when having sex without using a condom?** Boy age 15.

Dear 'Percentage seeker' – The chances of a girl getting pregnant if she doesn't use any form of contraception is around one in three every time she has sexual intercourse. Scary, isn't it? Unless, of course, you really want your girlfriend to get pregnant?

● **STOPPING THE EGG**

'The pill' is the main way of stopping an egg being released from the woman's ovary. The main type of pill is called the <u>combined</u> pill. This pill is great as long as you remember to take it, and it is even better if you use it with a condom to stop you getting nasty sexually transmitted bugs. There are other types of pills and injections which contain only one hormone called progesterone. Taking this hormone is not quite as effective as the combined pill.

Dear Dr Ann – **can you tell me about the contraceptive pill?** Age: 15 Sex: female.

Dear '15-year-old wanting to know about the contraceptive pill' – There are two types of contraceptive pill. The 'combined pill' is made up of two hormones – oestrogen and progesterone – and is almost 100% effective in stopping you getting pregnant if it is taken properly. It works by stopping the ovaries releasing an egg each month, so there is no egg to meet up with a sperm and develop into a baby. You need to take the pill every day for three weeks and then stop for a week, during which time you will have a bleed like a period. There is also another type of pill with only one hormone, called the 'progesterone-only pill' or 'mini pill'. This is slightly less effective, and you need to remember to take it the same time each day. Both types of pill have to be prescribed at your local GP practice or a family planning clinic. Before starting the pill, the doctor or nurse will go through all the advantages and disadvantages of the pill and make sure there is no medical reason for you not to take it. Remember, the pill does not stop sexually transmitted infections – so you do need to use condoms as well. To find out more and to obtain an excellent leaflet, contact the Family Planning Association – 0845 310 1334.

Dear Doctor Ann – **I'm on 'the pill' but I forgot to take it** so I took it 12 and a half hrs after I was meant to. What do I have to do to stop getting pregnant? 16 year old girl.

Dear 'Forgetful pill-taker' – It's best to take the pill at the same time each day, but there is some leeway. With the combined contraceptive pill, the cut-off point is 12 hours so you are probably OK. If you miss a pill for longer (or are on the 'progesterone-only pill'), you may need to take emergency contraception. If in doubt, ring one of the helplines such as 0800 0185 023 or 0845 310 1334 or your family doctor.

DEAD DODGY METHODS

The following methods of contraception are highly risky – but they are better than nothing:

- the <u>rhythm</u> method – not having sex when the woman is releasing an egg
- the <u>withdrawal</u> method – the man withdraws just before he comes

Dear doctor Ann – **hey is it possible to get pregnant if the man you are having sex with takes his penis out just before he ejaculates?**

Dear 'Living dangerously' – This is called the 'withdrawal' method but it doesn't really work. Yes, you definitely can get pregnant if the man takes his penis out before he comes. 'I promise I won't come inside you' is one of the most unreliable forms of contraception. Men often leak sperm from the tip of their penis before they actually come, and that sperm may well make you pregnant. Also, men do tend to get 'carried away' at the moment of orgasm and forget to do what they said they would! Don't forget about all those nasty sexually transmitted infections that could be avoided as well if he uses a condom.

● IN AN EMERGENCY

The <u>emergency contraceptive pill</u> contains progesterone hormones, which stop any fertilized egg from settling into the wall of your uterus (womb) and developing into a baby. It can be used more than once without a problem, but is not recommended as a regular form of contraception.

Dear Doctor Ann – **wot is the chance of getting pregnant if u use a conny and where can u get the emergency pill from** and can u take it just to be sure u r not pregnant and can some one get it 4 u – like can u take a m8s pill? 14 year old girl.

Dear 'Conny user' – A condom (conny) is a very good method of contraception, but it is not infallible. Sometimes it fails as a method because people take a chance and don't use one. Sometimes it breaks, sometimes it comes off, sometimes it's not put on properly, and sometimes it's not put on in time! So, lots of reasons why condoms can fail – but usually they do work very well. If any of these situations happen, you can use emergency contraception, which will work for up to 72 hours after the 'accident'. Emergency contraceptive pills are available from family planning and young person's clinics, from your family doctor or another GP – and they are free.

Chemists also sell them, but usually only if you're 16 or over. Get down to one of these places as quickly as possible – ideally within 24 hours of the condom 'trouble', OK within three days, and if you wait longer there are still ways you can be helped. You should really get your own pills as it's never good to use a mate's pill.

Dear Dr Ann – **After i have taken the morning after pill can i still be pregnant?** 15 year old girl.

Dear 'Can I still be pregnant after taking the morning-after pill' – Yes, you can still be pregnant even after taking the morning-after pill, otherwise known as 'emergency contraception'. However, it doesn't often happen, especially if you take it within 24 hours of having sex, when it is 96% effective. It shouldn't really be called the morning-after pill as it still works, though less well, up to three days after sex. If you take it within 48 hours (two days), it is 85% effective, and if you wait until three days (72 hours), it is 58% effective. After taking these pills, you may have a period immediately or, more often, at the usual time. If you do not bleed at either of these times, you should get checked out for being pregnant in case the pill hasn't worked. You can have a free pregnancy test from your family doctor, young people's or family planning clinic – or you can buy one from the chemist.

If all else goes wrong and you get pregnant, you have choices – but whatever you choose, you need to see a doctor quickly.

QUIZ 2 R U REALLY READY FOR IT ALL?

1 With girls' breasts

- a   all boys think that 'the bigger they come the better they are'
- b   they can go on growing till after you are 18 years old
- c   unlike the ones on 'models', girls' breasts actually come in all sorts of shapes and sizes and need to be lived with as they are

2 With girls' other 'bits':

- a   'labia' are like soft cushions on the outside of each side of the vaginal opening
- b   the 'clitoris' is the equivalent of a man's willy but smaller
- c   girls shouldn't go swimming when they have their periods

3 Masturbation is:

- a   bad for you
- b   will make boys run out of sperm for good if they do it too often
- c   something girls never, ever do

4 Sexual intercourse is:

- a   something you have to try before you get married
- b   only legal after you become 16 years of age
- c   boasted about by boys even if they haven't done it

5 When trying NOT to have babies:

- a   the boy taking his penis out before he 'comes' is a good method
- b   using a condom will stop you getting most nasty diseases from sex, as well as stopping you from having babies
- c   if you have to use 'emergency contraception', you have 72 hours, but the sooner the better

If you got all the answers right and you are over 16 – then you just *may* be ready for it. If you got all the answers wrong – your knobs and vaginas need to stay well apart.

Answers

1 **b and c** (girls' breasts come in all sizes; boys like breasts in all sizes)

2 **a and b** (girls and boys should know this)

3 **none of these answers are right** (so, relax both sexes and both hands)

4 **b and c** (but then boys boast about almost everything to do with sex)

5 **b and c** (if you are going to have sexual intercourse you'd better know this one)

Can I get

13

pregnant by...?

With all the modern forms of contraception
available, including emergency contraception, you
would think that there would be little chance of
anyone becoming pregnant if they didn't want to.
However, we all know that it does happen – 'Oh I
didn't know you could get pregnant that way' or 'I was
carried away by the heat of the moment' or 'I don't
know how it happened', etc. So you do need to know
how it *might* happen and try and avoid these
situations if humanly possible!

● **NOT RISKY**

Dear Doc Ann – **can you get pregnant from a boy's sperm by
swimming in the same swimming pool with him?** Girl aged 14.

Dear 'Swimming pool worrier' – No, no chance of you
getting pregnant from swimming in a swimming pool. Sperm

88

are not great survivors outside the human body, and the chlorine in the water of swimming pools would do for them good and proper.

Dear Doctor Ann – **can you become pregnant off a toilet seat?** Age: 13. Sex: female.

> *Dear 'Anxious about toilet seats'* – NO, NO, NO. If anyone tells you that's how they got pregnant, it's not true. Sperm are very fragile, tender little things and die very quickly on exposure to air – they don't survive on a toilet seat. You need to have sexual intercourse to get pregnant, or at least for the sperm to be near the entrance of the vagina.

RISKY

Hi Dr Ann – **can you get pregnant by getting fingered?** Girl aged 14.

> *Dear 'Finger worrier'* – The answer is technically yes, but unlikely. If you have been playing around with one another and your boyfriend has either actually 'come', or has produced some 'pre-cum', and he has got this on his fingers, and he either fingers you near the entrance to your vagina or actually puts his fingers into your vagina – then he may be putting his sperm somewhere where it can finally reach your eggs (ova) and you can get pregnant. All right – the chances are pretty low, but do you want to take the risk?

Dear Doctor Ann – **if I was masturbating the one day and the next day me and a girl was fooling around with no clothes on – can she have got pregnant?** 14 year old male.

Dear '14-year-old fooling around naked' – No, you cannot get a girl pregnant if you masturbate one day and fool around the next. BUT it does sound as though you are getting sexually aroused with your girlfriend in a way that could lead you into having sex itself (or as good as), when she would be at risk of getting pregnant. This is really risky – so best to get those clothes back on and talk to your girlfriend about what you are both doing. Realize that sex itself is worth waiting for, and it is also illegal under 16. If you carry on as you are, you should get some contraception sorted out. Meanwhile, if an accident happens, go and get emergency contraception as quickly as possible.

Dear Ann – **can you get pregnant from foreplay?** Girl aged 16.

Dear 'Getting pregnant during foreplay wonderer'– The simple answer is yes, there is some risk, but it is definitely much less risky than sexual intercourse itself. Sperm can survive for a very short time outside a woman's vagina, so that if a boy 'comes' and some sperm gets on your hands or near

your vaginal opening or onto your boyfriend's hands, and he touches you near your vaginal opening, there is just a chance (not worth taking) that some of his sperm might get into your vagina. So please just be careful as to where his sperm goes.

90

Dear Doc – **can you get pregnant if your bf has put the tip of his penis inside you?** I have heard that you can get pregnant with the wet bit that comes out of a boys willie before he actually 'comes' – is that true? Girl aged 16.

Dear 'Putting the tip inside' – **You can get pregnant, whether the tip or the whole of your bf's penis goes inside you – it's not just if he ejaculates when he is inside you. It is definitely true that you can get pregnant from the wet bit that comes out of a boy's willy before he actually comes. The 'pre-cum' that boys have coming out of their willy is meant to help as a lubricant when they are making love. But if you look at this so-called lubricant under a microscope, it sometimes contains some sperm too. This means that if the boy is using a condom, he needs to make sure he puts it on right at the beginning of making love, not just before he comes.**

● **VERY RISKY**

Hi doc – **can you get pregnant if you haven't had a period yet?** Age: 13. Sex: female.

Dear 'Can you get pregnant without periods? – **Yes, you can, so never have sex without using a condom and/or other form of contraception. You ovulate (produce eggs) before your period starts and this is about 14 days before the** period, and that can happen before you've ever had a period. But you absolutely should NOT be having sexual intercourse if you are 13 years old!

Dear Dr Ann – **can you become pregnant the first time you have sex?** Girl aged 15.

Dear 'Pregnancy wonderer' – You can get pregnant each and every time that you have sex, whether it is for the first time, the tenth time, the hundredth time or the thousandth time. Each time you have sexual intercourse without using any form of contraceptive protection, you have approximately a one in three chance of getting pregnant (to say nothing of the chance of catching a sexually transmitted disease – but that is a whole other ball game). That is a high, high chance! Please don't take it.

OK Doctor Ann – **about 2 weeks ago i had sex wiv my ex. He pulled out and I know this was a stupid thing to do but can I still get pregnant?** My period is 4 days late but my friend was saying its probably irregular because I've had to take the morning after pill before! Am i pregnant? Age: 14. Sex: female.

Dear 'Four days late' – Yes, you could be pregnant. Please go and get a pregnancy test to check this out – either from the chemist, or free from your doctor or a young people's clinic. Even though your boyfriend pulled out, a little bit of 'cum', which contains sperm, could have been released before he actually had an orgasm. It also sounds like it was a risky time of the month – though any time can be risky. If you've had to take the morning-after pill before, it seems like you need to really stop being 'stupid' and sort out some proper contraception. Get some condoms NOW – as you not only need to be protected against getting pregnant, but also from catching a sexually transmitted infection.

Help!

14

am I pregnant?

First, you need to know for sure whether you are pregnant or not, and then you need to make a decision as to whether you want to stay pregnant or not. Finding out whether you are pregnant or not is the easy bit. The decision as to whether you want to stay pregnant is much, much more difficult, so please, please know all about contraception before you start having sexual intercourse.

● **AM I PREGNANT?**

Dear Ann – **how do I know if I'm pregnant?** Age: 17. Sex: female.

Dear 'How do I know I'm pregnant' – The commonest first sign is missing a period when you have had sex. Sometimes, though not usually, you can still have a period, which is lighter than normal, even when you are pregnant. There are other signs of pregnancy, which include your breasts

getting bigger and feeling sick, which start to happen after a few weeks. If there is any risk you could be pregnant, get a pregnancy testing kit, either from the chemist, where you have to pay, or go and see your family doctor (GP) or a young person's or family planning clinic, where you can have a pregnancy test free.

Dear Doctor Ann – **2 weeks ago I slept with my friend's boyfriend. We were drunk and didn't use protection.** Because it was my friend's boyfriend I didn't tell anyone until the other day so I didn't get the morning after pill. My periods are now a week late and I'm really worried. I'm going to the Brook advisory clinic on Saturday but I wondered do I have to tell my parents if I need an abortion at 13? Girl aged 13.

> *Dear 'Drunken disaster'* – You are doing exactly the right thing by going to your local Brook Advisory Centre. Nobody, absolutely nobody likes having an abortion, and many abortions are avoidable by using the 'emergency contraceptive pill' within 72 hours of having unprotected sexual intercourse, so if it happens again, make sure you know all about taking the emergency contraceptive pill. You do not *have* to tell your parents about having an abortion, but although you may think they won't help you, after the initial reaction when they may be cross, they will help and support you. Talk to the people that you see at the Brook Advisory Centre about this and they will be able to advise you.

Sometimes, this can be a very difficult decision because there may be a great many different factors for you to take into account like:

• how old you are
• what you are doing with your life at the moment (school, exams, career, motherhood)
• how you feel about the child's father
• what your beliefs and feelings are about having an abortion, including your religious beliefs if you have a religion
• how you think your parents will react
• whether you think you are ready to start having babies
• who else there is around to help support you
• how you will continue with school work.

Dr Ann – I need help and dunno what to do – **I'm 3 months pregnant, and have told my parents about it and they don't want me to have an abortion,** but I don't think I can manage looking after a baby and think if I have it I will want to have it adopted. 14 year old girl.

Dear 'Dunno what to do' – What a difficult situation to find yourself in. Even if your parents might have different ideas about what you should do, I am sure it is a good idea that you have told them. In the final event, you have the right to decide for yourself and must not allow anyone to tell you what to do. I think some pregnancy counselling, by a doctor or counsellor, will help you make sense of things and help you sort out what the best thing is for you to do. It would probably also be a good idea to involve your parents in the counselling, as the counsellor or doctor should be able to help your relationship with your parents if you decide to have an abortion. If, however, you are thinking about having the baby, whether the baby's father is around or not, you will need a lot of support to finally decide whether to keep it or have it adopted. Whatever you decide, while you are pregnant, a doctor will arrange for you to have regular checks with a midwife to make sure that you and the baby keep healthy. The midwife should also put you in touch with social services, who can give advice about benefits, housing, and mother and baby units during your pregnancy. They can also put you in touch with an adoption agency, who will give you all the information you need about adoption. Once the baby has been legally adopted you cannot change your mind, but until then you can.

Help Doctor Ann – **I got raped and now I'm pregnant. Should I have an abortion or not?** Girl aged 14.

Dear 'Rape victim' – I am so, so sorry. This is a very difficult decision that you're having to face, and it would greatly help if you had someone to talk to about it. Can you talk to your parents, or do you have some close friend who you can discuss all your feelings with? Some of the things you will need to think about are: your own feelings about abortion, your religion and your religious feelings about abortion, how far pregnant you are, your age, your future education, the attitude of your parents, what other friends you have to support you through all this. You will also need help with the rape. If you do decide to have an abortion, you need to see a doctor – a general practitioner – or go to a young person's clinic or someone from a charitable abortion clinic like the Pregnancy Advisory Service. If the first doctor you see is not sympathetic, you have the right to consult another family doctor under these circumstances.

This doctor will refer you on to a second doctor, either at a local hospital or someone who is part of the abortion clinic set-up.

Facts about abortion

Abortion of foetuses up to the 24th week of pregnancy is legal in England, Scotland and Wales (in Northern Ireland it is only legal in exceptional circumstances).

- *abortion is available in these countries subject to the approval of two doctors*
- *the majority of abortions are carried out before 12 weeks*
- *legal abortion is very safe for the pregnant woman, and there is very little risk, particularly during early pregnancy*
- *legal abortion does not normally interfere with you having a baby later on in life*
- *legal abortion is free on the National Health Service in England, Scotland and Wales*

Useful organizations to help you decide:

- *your family doctor*
- *another family doctor of your choice*
- *The Brook Helpline 0800 0185 023*
- *Sexwise 0800 282930*
- *your local Family Planning Clinic (ring 0207 837 4044 to get information about how to contact them)*
- *British Pregnancy Advisory Service (BPAS) 08457 304030*

If you decide that you do want to be pregnant and that you do want to have the baby, then other people/organizations which may be useful are:

- *your family doctor*
- *another family doctor of your choice*
- *British Agency for Adoption and Fostering 0207 407 8800*

Doing it

having sex

HAVING FUN AND AVOIDING PROBLEMS

Although having sex itself is the most natural thing in the world, it is not always easy to begin with. Given that it is meant to be enjoyable and also meant to be by 'mutual consent' – which means that both partners agree to it on an equal basis – there can be many misunderstandings between people. Therefore, talking about it ahead of time is a very good idea.

● **AM I READY?**

Dear Dr Ann – **I met a boy on holiday and I really, really like him. He likes me too.** We want to meet up soon, but he keeps talking about getting the house to ourselves so that we can have some 'fun'. I'm not naive enough to think he wants to play 'houses', but know he probably will want to have sexual intercourse with me. What shall I do? 15 year old girl.

Dear 'Holiday romancer' – The first thing to do is to decide on what kind of relationship you want to have with this boy.

Why don't you sit down over coffee or something (well away from temptation to actually do anything together) and discuss exactly what his ideas of 'fun' are? This will show him that you take the question of sex seriously. You may then want to tell him that you don't want to have sex yet. You can also point out that as you are only 15, it is illegal for him to have sexual intercourse with you. You can then see how he reacts to this and take it from there.

NO ENTRY

Dear Doctor Ann – **is it illegal for two people under the age of 16 to have sex together?** Boy aged 15.

Dear 'Sex under 16' – Yes, it is, and although it is unlikely that the police will get involved, many people who have sex early do regret it. The best things are worth waiting for. Meanwhile, try the other sexy things you can do without actually having sexual intercourse.

Dear Doctor Ann – **my girlfriend recently asked me if I wanted to have sex and I do** but I'm afraid I will make a fool of myself and not know what to do. Age: 14. Sex: male.

Dear '14-year-old wanting to have sex' – Sometimes you want to do things very young, when you should really wait because it is much better later. You don't say how old your girlfriend is, but if she is under the age of 16, then what you are doing is illegal anyway. Older teenagers who have had sex at your age say that they regret having started to have sex so young. If you ignore this advice and decide to go ahead, please use a condom because it will protect you against sexually transmitted diseases and will help protect your girlfriend from getting pregnant. As far as 'making a fool of yourself' – again, if you wait, you will know more about what to do when it does actually happen.

● WHAT IS ALL THIS SEX STUFF?

Dear Doctor Ann – **how can you tell whether you've lost your virginity or not?** Girl aged 15.

Dear 'Unsure about being a virgin'– This means that you have had actual sexual intercourse with a boy and he has put his penis into your vagina. A sign of being a virgin used to be that your hymen, which is a very thin layer of skin that normally covers the entrance to the vagina of a girl from birth, had not been torn by having sexual intercourse. However, girls can lose their hymens in other ways – like riding bicycles or horses, but this does not mean that they are not virgins. Boys are considered to have 'lost their virginity' the first time that they have sexual intercourse.

Dear Doctor Ann – **I feel a bit silly asking you Dr Ann what an orgasm is? Is it bad? What do you do when you have an orgasm??** Boy aged 14.

Dear 'Orgasm wonderer' – You should never feel silly asking someone to explain anything that you don't understand. There are probably lots of people reading this who also may not know what an orgasm is, but are too shy to ask. An orgasm is the feeling that occurs when you get very sexually excited. It is also known as a 'climax' or 'coming'. What normally happens when men and women get sexually excited is that the sexual excitement gets greater and greater till suddenly there is an overwhelming feeling of pleasure. At this point, the man normally ejaculates semen from the end of his penis, and in women there is a tightening of the walls of their vagina. After an orgasm, sexual excitement fades away and is followed by a general nice feeling of completeness. When men and women make love, they do not normally have orgasms at exactly the same time, but when they do, it is extremely nice. Men and women don't always have an orgasm every time they get sexually excited.

Hi doctor Ann – **How do you have sex as I have a boyfriend and we are going to sleep together.** Does it hurt? Do you have to help a boy put a condom on as I have never done this before. 17 year old girl.

Dear '17-year-old wanting to know about how to have sex' – I am sure that you know that having sexual intercourse involves the boy putting his erect penis into your vagina. It does sometimes take a bit of practice to get it right – so don't rush things. It is possible that it may hurt you the first time, or even the first few times. Some of this hurting may be because you still have an intact 'hymen' (the bit of skin covering the entrance to your vagina that may get gently torn a bit when your boyfriend tries to put his penis into you). So get him to take it easy and be gentle. Your boyfriend does need to wear a condom, especially if you are not using any other form of contraception (like the pill), but whether he puts it on himself, or you put it on him, is up to you – just make sure that he is wearing one!

Dear Doctor Ann – this might sound a bit silly but I really am desperate to know. **I'm not a virgin I've had sex once. But I still don't know what penetration is – can you help?** 15 year girl.

> *Dear 'Curious about penetration'* – The word 'penetration', when used in a sexual context, means a boy has actually put his penis into the girl's vagina. It doesn't make any difference how *far* he has put it in – it can mean even just the tip of his penis.

● HAVING A BIT OF A PROBLEM

Dear Dr Ann – **I have a long term b/f and we decided to have sex but he couldn't get his penis into me.** Is it possible to fix this??? 17 year old girl.

> *Dear 'Couldn't get it in'* – There are many reasons why this may happen. Probably there is nothing to fix and it will just happen with a bit of practice. There are some simple things to do, like checking you are wet enough before he tries to put his penis into you.

Dear Dr Ann – please can you help me. **I have been going out with my boyfriend for ages now and we still haven't had sex. He usually gets too nervous** and says he can't do it or that he can't stop to put a condom on. He knows it's all in his head but what do i do to help him? 17 year old girl.

Dear 'Person wanting to help her boyfriend' – This is quite a common problem with boys. They want to have sex, but they get so anxious about it, nothing happens. It does not mean he does not love you, but it may mean that he is still anxious about doing the right thing. The best way of helping him is to respect him and be very patient indeed. He needs to stop worrying about it – because it will all be fine in the long run. Stick to all the sexy things that you can do without actually having sexual intercourse, and then one day things will just 'happen' OK. And of course, do sort out the contraception first.

COOLING IT/SLOWING DOWN

Dear Doctor Ann – **I have been having sex for a while now but I have not been that bothered about doing it and I want to know how to stop my boyfriend from pressurizing me into it.** I don't even like doing it. 16 year old girl.

Dear 'Wanting to say no' – I think that you need to have a proper discussion with your boyfriend about this at some time when you are free from any chance of having sex – say over supper sometime, or over coffee. You need to explain to him how you feel, and also explain that it will really interfere with your relationship if he makes you feel bad about not having sex when you don't want to. If he is the slightest bit sensitive, this will be OK by him. Also, suggest to him that there may be moments when he doesn't want to have sex, and you will respect that too.

It's catching

16

and it could be you!

SEXUALLY TRANSMITTED DISEASES AND WHAT TO DO ABOUT THEM

Sexually transmitted infections (STIs) or sexually transmitted diseases (STDs) are the same thing. They are a group of infections that are mainly spread from one person to another during sexual intercourse. The reason for worrying about them is because (a) many of them are painful; (b) they can make you ill; (c) some of them can cause a woman not to be able to have a baby; (d) some of them can kill you.

● HOW ARE THEY CAUGHT?

Dear Doctor Ann – **What are STDs?** boy aged 15.

Dear 'Curious about STDs' – These initials stand for Sexually Transmitted Diseases (sometimes also called STIs, which stands for Sexually Transmitted Infections). They are types of infections that are caught by having sexual intercourse, though some can be caught by other sexual activities. There are a whole lot of different ones, usually caused by bugs called viruses or bacteria. These include: chlamydia, trichomonas, gonorrhoea, human immunodeficiency virus (HIV), herpes, etc. If you think you might have caught one of these, please do go and get checked by a doctor. Most, but not all of them, can be easily cured and, if dealt with quickly, will not cause any damage or be passed on to other people. Some of these diseases that are caught sexually, such as thrush, can also occur without sexual contact.

Dear Dr Ann – **would you get a disease if you had sex for the first time without protection?** Age: 15. Sex: female.

Dear 'Wondering about getting diseases from unprotected sex' – Yes, I'm afraid you can, if the person you have sex with has a sexually transmitted infection such as chlamydia, gonorrhoea, genital warts or HIV – and he may not even know he has an STI or tell you if he does know. So please make sure you don't have sex without using a condom. Don't be afraid to ask your partner about what he has been up to sexually before. If you know him well enough to be having sex, then you should know him well enough to ask questions.

● COULD I HAVE CAUGHT ONE OF THOSE STIs?

Dear Doctor Ann – **I have pain when peeing and an itchy vagina** after having a holiday 1 nite stand a couple of weeks ago, could i have an STI? Girl age 15 years 11 months.

Dear 'Could I have an STI?' – Yes, you certainly could have an STI and I suggest you go and see a doctor – either your GP

105

or your nearest GUM (genito-urinary medicine) clinic, to get tested as soon as possible. Remember, what you tell a doctor is confidential, which means they won't tell anyone else unless you give permission. You may have cystitis, caused by a bacteria in the bladder or urethra, and/or thrush, which is a yeast infection. These are both easily treated by taking some antibiotics or anti-yeast treatment. BUT there are various sexually transmitted infections that you could also have caught, including chlamydia, trichomonas, gonorrhoea, let alone HIV, as STIs tend to hunt in packs. The first three and many others are easily treated, so please get tested and don't have any more sex until it is all sorted out or you may be passing it on to someone else.

● HERPES, THRUSH, CHLAMYDIA, WARTS

Dear Doctor Ann – **I really want to snog my boyfriend** but i have never done it before so I want it to be special and I want to now. **But he always seems to have cold sores.** I still wanna snog the face off him. Age: 13. Sex: female.

Dear 'Desperate to snog your boyfriend' – I can understand that you want to snog your boyfriend, but I would wait until his cold sores have cleared up before doing this. Cold sores are caused by the herpes virus, which is contagious, and it might mean that you end up with cold sores yourself. Unfortunately, once you catch this virus it can stay in the system and come back every so often. By the way, *any* part of you that gets kissed by someone who has a cold sore may get infected by the herpes virus. Also, if you want to help your boyfriend, suggest that he can get some special anti-herpes cream from the chemist.

Dear Doctor Ann – **I think I might have a yeast infection.** Can you please tell me the symptoms? 14 year old girl.

> *Dear 'Possible yeast infection sufferer' –* I presume you think you have a yeast infection in your genital area. The commonest one of these is called 'thrush'. It makes you want to itch and scratch and, if you look down there with a mirror, it will be all red. If it is in the vagina itself, then you may notice a white curdy discharge. Sometimes a yeast infection occurs after taking a course of antibiotics, or it can be linked to sex. It's best if you can talk to your mum, but whatever the cause, do go and get checked out. That way you really know what it is and can get the right treatment – either on prescription or you can buy an anti-yeast cream over the counter from a chemist.

Dear Doctor Ann – **can you die from chlamydia?** Girl aged 16.

> *Dear 'Chlamydia worrier' –* No, you can't die from it, but it is a sneaky bacteria in that you don't always know that you have got it. You catch it during sexual intercourse without a condom (it is a sexually transmitted infection). It causes different problems in men and women. In men, it can cause soreness of the tube in their penises which they pee through (the urethra), so it hurts to pee. In women, it can cause an inflammation in the tubes which carry the egg from the ovary down to the uterus (fallopian tubes) and can damage them so they get blocked which might mean that the woman can't have babies. It can also cause inflammation of the neck of the woman's womb and give a vaginal discharge. If you have had sex without a condom and could have caught it (or any other STIs) – get checked by a doctor as it is easily treated with antibiotics.

Rough guide to sexually transmitted infections

Boys:

- 👁 *Gunk or blood coming out of your penis – think **gonorrhoea, non-specific urethritis or chlamydia***
- 👁 *Warty lumps on your penis or near it – think **genital warts***
- 👁 *Painful sores or blisters on your penis or near it – think **herpes***
- 👁 *An itchy penis with a red tip – think **thrush***
- 👁 *Itchy scrotum and pubic hair – think **crabs***

Girls:

- 👁 *If your vaginal discharge goes thick, gooey, smelly, itchy, a different colour... then you might have **thrush or trichomonas***
- 👁 *If it hurts to pee, then think **cystitis** – but it could be **thrush***
- 👁 *If you get warty lumps around the vagina – think **genital warts***
- 👁 *If your vagina itches or gets sore – think **thrush***
- 👁 *Chlamydia can cause cystitis, discharge, soreness – or nothing at all!*

Dear Doctor Ann – **I have got some wart type lumps on my penis.** Boy aged 16.

Dear 'Warty penis owner' – The standard normal post-pubertal human penis comes with many different types of lumps and bumps, most of which are entirely innocent. What are *not* warts, but just part of your normal equipment, are the kind of bumps you get all over your scrotal bag, with hairs growing out of them. They are slightly raised, whitish lumps, about 1 millimetre in diameter, that are mainly on the underside of your penis.

All warts, wherever they are, are caused by a virus. Eighty per cent of the warts will disappear within a year without you doing anything about them, and most of them don't do any harm. However, there is a worry about passing on warts from penises to vaginas because in women, there is some link between certain types of wart virus and getting cancer of the cervix (neck of the womb) in later life. So, if you think that you have got warts, get them checked out, as you can get a 'paint' for them which helps them go away. Best (as always) to use a condom if you are having sexual intercourse.

● AIDS AND HIV

Dear Doctor Ann — I have read about HIV in many places now but I am unsure about something. **If you both have a test and you both don't have HIV is it still possible to get it?** I mean if you come into contact with her blood or something? 17 year old boy.

Dear 'Unsure about HIV' – The commonest way that people in the UK catch HIV is by having sexual intercourse with someone who has already been infected by the virus. This can be between a man and woman or between two men. It can also be caught by using a needle to inject drugs which has been used by someone who has the infection or the disease. HIV is a nasty, nasty virus, as although there are treatments available which slow the virus down, as yet there is no way of completely curing people with Aids and most people do eventually die from it. If you both have negative HIV tests and you have not been in contact with anyone with HIV for at least three months (as it can take this time for a test to become positive), there is no way you can catch HIV from her. But if you are having sex with this person, please still use condoms to protect yourself against other sexually transmitted infections.

Like attracted
to like

AM I GAY OR LESBIAN?

Most people are sexually attracted to someone of the opposite sex to themselves. This is OK as the main point of having sex is to have babies. However, there are also men and women who mainly enjoy having sex with someone of the same sex as themselves and they are known as homosexual, gay or, if it is a woman attracted to another woman, lesbian. Other people enjoy having sex with someone of the opposite sex and with someone of the same sex, and this is known as being bisexual.

● **BOYS TURNED ON BY BOYS**

Dear Doctor – **I think I'm gay what should I do?** Boy aged 13.

Dear '13-year-old who thinks he is gay' – Give yourself a chance. There is no absolutely foolproof way of telling whether you are homosexual or not, and anyhow, usually it will not be as definite as that – some people may find that they are, at one time or other, sexually attracted both to people of the opposite sex and to people of the same sex. At 13, your sex hormones that turn on your puberty and your sexual drive have recently kicked in. Many boys, when they are going through puberty, quite fancy other boys – especially if they are surrounded by friends who are boys. About one in every 25 men aged 16 to 19 report having had a homosexual experience. But the number of older men who end up gay is even lower. Wait a bit before deciding whether you are heterosexual or gay.

Dear Doctor Ann – **I think that my boyfriend is gay!** what should I do? 15 year old girl.

Dear 'Girl with possibly gay boyfriend' – The answer is simple – stay his friend and let him talk about it. Don't feel that you are going to 'rescue him' from gayness though. When boys go through puberty, their hormones are rushing around in a quite confused way, and some boys find that they are temporarily attracted to other boys as well as to girls. As things settle down, most of them become attracted to girls, and only relatively few (less than 3 in 100 if the research about it is to be believed) stay gay. If he is one of these – then fine, but you won't change him.

Hi Dr – **I am a 14 year old boy and I am a bit concerned about the possibility that I might be a homosexual.** I am attracted to girls as much as any man, yet sometimes I feel slight attractions toward members of the same sex. Nothing serious, just very slight. Am I gay?

Dear 'Worried about being homosexual' – No problems here. It is extremely common for 14-year-olds to be attracted to both sexes – probably because it is soon after puberty when your hormones are making you feel sexually interested anyhow! If you are already finding that girls are attractive, it is very likely that you will end up by being a heterosexual, which means enjoying having sex with girls.

Hi Doctor Ann – **I am worried because people are all calling me gay and stuff coz my voice has not broken.** I'm NOT gay, why do they say this?? Help! Boy aged 15.

Dear 'Voice not broken yet' – For some reason people love teasing other people and don't realize how much it hurts. Ignore them and the teasing is likely to stop. I can guarantee your voice will break sometime soon. In any case, your voice breaking/not breaking has absolutely nothing to do with who you are sexually attracted to.

Dear Doctor Ann – **i am a 14 year old boy and i am very worried if i am gay or not?** i have a girlfriend and i am attracted to girls but recently i have felt attracted to boys also. It's been playing on my mind for nearly 6 months now and i'm not sure if it is a phase or not. i hope to god it is because I would hate the thought of being gay. Please give me some advice.

Dear 'Worried about being gay' – This kind of concern is very common when you are going through puberty and developing sexually. Only a small percentage of boys who have the feelings that you describe will, in fact, end up gay, and a small number of people will also be bisexual, which means you actually have sexual feelings for men and women. There is no right or wrong in all this – just the way that you are.

● GIRLS TURNED ON BY GIRLS

Dear Ann – **I attend an all girls school. It is a boarding school and I share a dormitory with two girls and they're both lesbians.** Most nights they sleep together but last night they got into my bed. To start with they started hugging and kissing me. But soon they were feeling my breasts. At this point i pushed them off. I am straight. I tried to talk to a teacher but they just said I was lying. They said this because I used to be a trouble maker in lessons. Please help. Girl aged 14.

Dear 'Boarder having trouble with other girls at school' – I think that your experience at your school is not that uncommon at single-sex boarding schools. I am sorry that the school did not help you out. The problem is that having only girls or boys of the same sex around when all those hormones are bursting through during puberty makes it almost inevitable that some will let out their sexual feelings on those immediately around them. It does sound as if you handled the situation extremely well. Keep on telling them that you are not interested, or ask to move dormitories.

Dear Doctor Ann – **hi I'm Gay and the thing is I really like one of my best friends.** I haven't told her how I feel coz I'm afraid to lose her friendship which means a great deal to me. However sometimes I feel really sad and just want to tell her how I feel. 16 year old female.

Dear 'Girl who is gay' – I assume when you say that you really 'like' one of your best friends, you are actually saying that you are sexually attracted to her? You may be right in keeping this to yourself, because if you reveal how you feel, she may feel pressurized by your feelings. On the other hand, it might help you to gently discuss your feelings with her, but also to say that you are not expecting her to feel the same way. Research suggests that only about two in every hundred women actually have a sexual experience with another girl when they are aged between 16 and 19.

● WANTING TO CHANGE SEX

Dear Doctor Ann – **since i was about 9 i have wanted to be a boy.** I know it sounds strange and i don't think it is just a phase i am going through because i feel very strongly about it. I just really want to be a boy and when i think about how i will never be able to it gets me down and makes me feel depressed, is there anything i can do to stop me feeling this way?? please help. 14 year old girl.

Dear 'Girl who wants to be a boy' – I think that you need to talk to someone about this. I would suggest that your family doctor, or another doctor in the same practice (if you are too shy to see your own doctor), would be a good place to start. At 14 you are too young to decide on changing your sex. But there is no harm in discussing it with an expert. Have you talked to your parents or some close friend about your feelings?

Lots of young people think that they might be gay. It can make you feel quite isolated if you can't talk about it. If you want to talk about it further, why not ring the Lesbian and Gay Switchboard on 0207 837 7324. You won't have to give your name.

Your body

belongs
to you

BEING SEXUALLY HARASSED, MANIPULATED OR ABUSED, AND STOPPING IT

Sometimes you can know someone for a long time and like them a lot and then they'll start to pressurize you to do things you don't like at all. But since you like that person and he's/she's always been nice to you before, you don't like to ask him/her to stop. But you can and you should stop them. You don't have to let anyone do anything to you that you do not like, even if it is someone in your own family, a long-term friend or a neighbour, or an adult you've always got on well with.

● **FEELING THE PRESSURE**

Dear Doctor Ann – **I really like this guy at the moment and I want to snog him but he has a reputation of telling people when they are bad kissers** and i'm really worried about being a bad kisser. Also he is a lot more advanced than me and I'm worried he will want more. 14 year old female.

115

Dear 'Wanting to snog a guy with a reputation' – You need to make up your mind what it is that you really want. You needn't worry about being a 'bad kisser'. Kissing is not some kind of competition like running a race. It is a sign of real affection and that you really care for someone. So, the 'best' kissers are not always the ones who get the most practice, but the ones that are most able to express their feelings for the other person. This will apply to the guy that you 'really like'. If he is telling people that they are 'bad kissers', then he is not worth knowing because he is abusing those people's trust and affection for him.

Hi Doctor – **I have a problem with this boy in my class who is really nice but he always feels me up in class** like putting his hand on my knee and he wants me to touch his #!@%!! And he always asks if I will shag him and stuff like that!! 13 year old female.

Dear 'Person having a problem with a boy in class' – Don't think that this is your fault in any way. It sounds as if this boy isn't very nice and is harassing you – he needs to be stopped. It is absolutely right to say loudly and firmly 'No – I don't want this and you MUST STOP IT'. Tell him he is being crap and talk to your teacher about it if he goes on.

Dear Dr Ann – **I'm a 17 year old virgin who is abstaining from sex till after marriage.** I've had 1 boyfriend in my entire life since I was 11 and he wants sex but I can't and he says stuff about sex being natural and that eventually us two will get married. Should I give in? 17 year old girl.

Dear 'Being asked to give in' –
Don't do what you don't think is right for you. You are in control of your life and your body. If you want to stay a virgin till you get married, then please, please stick to that. If you give in to him over this, you may regret it for ever. So wait till you get married if that is what you want.

Dear Doctor Ann – **should I keep my boyfriend who's 19 happy by having sex with him?** I know i shouldn't do anything I don't want to do but i love him and I'm scared in case i lose him. Age: 15. Sex: female.

Dear 'Scared about losing boyfriend' –
It sounds like you really aren't ready to have sex with this boyfriend even if you do think you love him. There's absolutely no guarantee that you will keep your boyfriend even if you do have sex with him. You should also remember that it's illegal for him to be having sex with you until you are 16.

Dear Ann – it's accepted that if a girl does not want to do a particular thing with her boyfriend then she just has to say NO, and there's no real questions asked. If it's the boy who wants to go slower why is it a bigger deal, and why do they always make u feel bad about it later? Boy aged 16.

Dear 'Boy wanting to say NO' – Nobody should be putting pressure on you to have sex when you don't want to, for whatever reason, whether you are a boy or a girl. It is not a big deal, just very sensible. Anyone who makes you feel bad for saying 'NO' or 'NOT YET' is a bully, and even if it is difficult, don't give into this bullying. It certainly does not mean you don't fancy the person concerned.

NO ENTRY

● WHEN THINGS GET SERIOUSLY NASTY

Dear Dr Ann – **can u b abused by another teenager?** or am i just being stupid and imagining things? 15 year old boy.

Dear 'Can u b abused by another teenager' – I am not sure whether your question means sexually, physically or mentally abused. Sadly, in all cases the answer is yes – and if you think this is happening to you or a friend, don't keep it to yourself. Please tell someone you trust – your mother, father, sister, teacher, aunt or uncle? Or if you really feel that is not possible, please phone Childline on 0800 1111.

Dear Doctor Ann – **about 6 months ago I waz being stalked by a boy in our class.** He rang my house every 5 minutes and made friends with my brothers so they invited him round. When he waz round my house he would come in my room and force me onto my bed and say this is what u want isn't it? 13 year old girl.

Keep Out

Dear 'Stalked 13-year-old' – This boy is really bad news. The rest of your family need to know what he is doing and they need to stop inviting him round. If someone is ever bothering you, and you don't want them to go on, but you can't manage to stop them, or you can't stay out of their way – then you should tell someone who you think can help. It might be your mother, a teacher, an older sister, a close friend, a doctor. If you tell one person and they don't believe you, or are too frightened to help you, then try someone else and keep on telling till you find someone who will help you. Also, tell your friends so that they can stay away from that person, and your friends' parents may help you too.

Dear Doctor Ann – **There's a boy we know who is really rough when he's having sex and often makes people do it with him.** He doesn't physically force them, it's persuasion. How can we stop him? 4 girls aged 15.

Dear 'Four girls knowing rough boy' – This sounds like very nasty bullying to me and bullies should not be allowed to get their own way. Why don't you girls discuss it together and 'gang up' against him and tell him to stop or you will tell. Otherwise, tell an adult in the school about it and make sure he is stopped.

Dear Doctor Ann – **my boyfriend keeps pushing me into sleeping with him** what should i say to him? 13 year girl.

119

Dear '13-year-old being pressured by boyfriend' – First and foremost, it is totally illegal for your boyfriend to have sex with you. At 13 you are way under the legal age of consent. Say 'absolutely no'. He has no right at all to 'push you' into sleeping with him. If you don't want to sleep with him, whatever your age, then he should take 'no' as 'no'. If he keeps on at you about having sex with him, tell someone you trust about what is happening and ditch him.

Dear Doc – my mum and dad separated when I was a baby and I never see my dad. **I now have a new stepdad who I like but he keeps wanting me to really cuddle up to him and all that which I don't like,** and I don't know whether to tell my mum. 14 year old girl.

Dear 'Don't know whether to tell your mum' – I can quite understand that you may be finding it difficult to tell your mum, especially if nothing has actually happened. But it does sound as if he is going too far. Your mum is the best person for you to talk to and she should talk to him about it all. If you can't tell your mum, or she doesn't take what you say seriously, you should try and tell another adult who you trust, like a teacher, school nurse, or your family doctor.

Dear Doctor Ann – **My friend is having a relationship with an older man and he beats her and treats her bad** but she won't leave him i am thinking of telling her parents and i don't know what to say 'cos this man has also made a pass at me and i don't know what to do. 14 year old female.

Dear 'Person with a badly treated friend' – If a friend tells you that they are being bullied or made to do something they do not want to, then do try and help them in whatever way you can, otherwise she will feel very alone with her problem. She has probably started to think things like 'this must be all my own fault because I am letting it happen to me', but she must not be allowed to think like that. This older man is at fault. Make absolutely sure that you yourself stay away from this man and tell an adult who you can trust about what is going on. I would suggest discussing it with your own parents first and let them tell your friend's parents about what is going on. If you can't tell your parents, then maybe there is a teacher at school or a relative of yours who you can talk to about it. It will be difficult for you, I know, but you really need to help your friend, and protect yourself.

● RAPE

Dear Doctor Ann – **I was raped by one of my mates.** He is usually really nice but when I was drunk one night and he was he did it. It was when I was lying down and tired and I felt him inside me. I didn't want to say anything though because I was scared. What can I do? 14 year old female.

Dear 'Person who was raped by a mate' – This sounds like what is called 'date rape', where you knew the boy as a friend but he forced himself on you. 'Date rape' is a crime, just like any other kind of rape. If you haven't told anyone about it, then try telling someone you really trust. If you can't do that, then write down everything that happened – you may find that just writing it down helps because it sort of puts it 'outside' you and then you may find you can tell someone else about it. You yourself have done absolutely nothing wrong, but you should get checked in case you are pregnant or have caught a sexually transmitted disease.

Dear Dr Ann – **I was raped, and I got pregnant. I really want to have an abortion, but I can't tell my parents.** Is there any way at all I could have an abortion without them knowing. I know what will happen, and I'm OK with that. I just can't cope with a rapist's baby. My parents don't know I was raped. I'm 13.

Dear '13-year-old girl who was raped' – You must be feeling awful and very frightened. You MUST get some help as quickly as possible. It is possible to have an abortion without telling your parents, but I am sure they will support you if you do tell them, and that will be a great support to you. Meanwhile, tell a school nurse, a teacher you trust, or your family doctor and they will not only be able to help but will help you tell your parents. Apart from being pregnant, you will also need to be checked to make sure you have not caught any sexually transmitted infection, and you will need some support related to the rape. If you do want an abortion, the sooner you have it the safer it is.

QUIZ 3 WHAT SEX HAS GOT FOR YOU?

1 Can a girl get pregnant...
- [ ] a off a lavatory seat?
- [ ] b even if the boy only puts the tip of his willy into a girl's vagina?
- [ ] c the very first time she has sexual intercourse?

2 Is it true that...
- [ ] a the difference between love and herpes is that herpes lasts for ever?
- [ ] b there is now a cure for Aids?
- [ ] c once you have a wart on your willy, it will stay there for ever?

3 What are the best ways of NOT getting a sexually transmitted disease...
- [ ] a not having sex
- [ ] b doing sexy things that you like without having sexual intercourse
- [ ] c using a condom whenever you have sexual intercourse?

4 Is it true that...
- [ ] a you can tell whether you are gay/lesbian at the age of 14 years?
- [ ] b one in fourteen boys have had some kind of gay experience?
- [ ] c after one gay experience you will always be gay?

5 When a person is sexually harassed...
- [ ] a the person harassed is to blame
- [ ] b they should always try and talk about it to someone they can trust
- [ ] c they should always say 'no' loudly and clearly

If you got all the answers right – brilliant! You are street and sex wise.

If you got all the answers wrong – read this book again so that you know the right answers before you get into TROUBLE!!!

Answers

1 **b and c** (Know your facts and you will stay away from having babies till you want them)

2 **a** (herpes infections do tend to hang around!)

3 **a, b and c** (condoms do stop the nasties – so use them)

4 **none of these** (because a boy is attracted to other boys doesn't necessarily mean they will be gay as adults)

5 **b and c** (don't keep it a secret if someone is doing something you don't want)

Need to find out more?

Teenage Health Freak

*The Diary of a Teenage Health Freak
(3rd edition, OUP 2002)*
The book that got it all going. Read the latest version of Pete Payne's celebrated diary in all its gory detail, to find out pretty much all you need to know about your health, your body and how it works (or doesn't – whatever).

*The Diary of the Other Health Freak
(3rd edition, OUP 2002)*
The book that kept it all going. Pete's sister Susie set out to outshine her big brother with a diary of her own, bringing the feminine touch to a huge range of teenage issues – sex, drugs, relationships, the lot.

Teenage Health Freak websites

www.teenagehealthfreak.org
www.doctorann.org
Two linked websites for young people. Catch up on the daily diary of Pete Payne, age 15 – still plagued by zits, a dodgy sex life, a pestilent sister... Jump to Doctor Ann's virtual surgery for all you want to know about fatness and farting, sex and stress, drinking and drugs, pimples and periods, hormones and headaches, and a million other things.

Other websites for teenagers

BBC kid's health
www.bbc.co.uk/health/kids

Mind Body Soul
www.mindbodysoul.gov.uk

Lifebytes
www.lifebytes.gov.uk

All your problems

ChildLine
Studd Street, London N1 0QW
Freepost 1111, London N1 0BR
Tel: 0207 239 1000
Helpline: 0800 1111
(24 hours a day,
every day of the year)
www.childline.org.uk
Provides a national telephone helpline for children and young people in danger or distress, who want to talk to a trained counsellor. All calls are free and confidential.

Bullying

Anti-Bullying Campaign
185 Tower Bridge Road,
London SE1 2UF
Tel: 0207 378 1446
Gives telephone advice for young people who are being bullied. There are also some websites where you can get help...

Bullying Online
www.bullying.co.uk

Pupiline
www.pupilline.com

If you are ill
NHS Direct
Tel: 0845 46 47
www.nhsdirect.nhs.uk
Talk to a nurse on the phone about any health problem you are worried about.

HIV/AIDS
National Aids Helpline
Tel: 0800 567123
(free and confidential; available 24 hours a day, 7 days a week)
Questions or worries about Aids can be discussed with a trained adviser.

Sex and everything attached
Brook Advisory Service
Young people's helpline:
0800 0185 023
www.brook.org.uk
User-friendly information service, offering advice on sex and contraception for all young people. Will tell you all about local clinics and send you leaflets even if you are under 16.

fpa (formerly The Family Planning Association)
2–12 Pentonville Road,
London N1 9FP

Tel: 0207 837 5432
Helpline: 0845 310 1334 (9am–7pm, Mon–Fri)
Gives information on all aspects of contraception and sexual health. Free fun leaflets available. They also run a telephone helpline for anyone who wants information on contraception and sexual health. Phone the helpline number to find your nearest fpa clinic.

BAAF (British Agencies for Adoption and Fostering)
Tel: 0207 593 2000
(9am–5pm, Mon–Fri)
www.baaf.org.uk
A central agency for organizations involved in adoption and fostering. Publishes useful information leaflets and books about various aspects of adoption. Offers advice on tracing.

Rape Crisis Helplines
Look in the telephone directory or ring Directory Enquiries on 192 for the Helpline number in your area. Provide free confidential support and advice to victims of rape.

Lesbian and Gay Switchboard
Tel: 0207 837 7324 (24 hours a day)
www.llgs.org.uk
(This is the London and national switchboard; there are also a number of regional switchboards.)
Offers information and advice to lesbians and gay men and their families and friends.

Index